P9-DMI-751

Easy Microwave Preserving

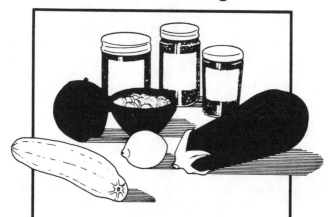

The shortcut way to
jams, jellies, fruits, sauces,
pickles, chutneys, relishes,
salsas, blanching vegetables,
drying herbs and
special extras!

**by Cynthia Fischborn
and Cheryl Long**

Culinary Arts Ltd.

Original cover art by Susan Parsley White, L-Grafix
Interior art by Robert Francis
Edited by Lee Jewell

Revised Second Printing © 1989
Copyright © 1988
By Cynthia Fischborn and Cheryl Long

All rights reserved. No part of this book may be reproduced in any
form or by any means without written permission from the publishers.

Library of Congress Cataloging-in-Publication Data

Fischborn, Cynthia, date.
    Easy Microwave Preserving.

        Includes index.
        1. Food — Preservation.   2. Microwave cookery.
I. Long, Cheryl.   II. Title.
TX601.F58 1988   641.4'2 87-5236
ISBN 0-914667-08-4

Printed in the United States of America

Published by:
Culinary Arts Ltd.
P.O. Box 2157
Lake Oswego, Oregon 97035
Books by Culinary Arts Ltd.:
    How To Make Danish Fruit Liqueurs
    Gourmet Vinegars: How To Make And Cook With Them
    Gourmet Mustards: How To Make And Cook With Them
    Easy Microwave Preserving
    Classic Liqueurs: The Art Of Making And Cooking With Liqueurs

Publisher's catalog available upon request.

TABLE OF CONTENTS

INTRODUCTION

The two of us have been enthusiatic microwave cooks, both professionally and at home, for many years. We've tried to cook almost anything edible in our microwave ovens!

Since one thing generally leads to another, we found ourselves writing a microwave magazine. There was a surprising response from our readers to any of our microwave preserving recipes and tips. Once a brief local television appearance showing how to make our **EASY BERRY LOW-SUGAR FREEZER JAM** drew over 500 recipe request letters!

These experiences, along with the urgings of our microwave cooking students, made us aware of the tremendous need for a book about microwave preserving. This book is a collection of our best recipes, tips and techniques. It is also, we believe, the first book on the subject.

The world of microwave cooking is one of continuing expansion. New products, techniques, recipes and, not least of all, breakthroughs in microwave technology continue to take place. Thus as our book begins a new chapter in microwave cooking, it is just that, a beginning. Be assured that we will be continuing to test and experiment with both recipes and technology of the future and shall, when appropriate, update this book. We would be happy to hear from you on this subject. Our sincere wish is that you find this cookbook the resource you have been looking for.

ABOUT THE AUTHORS

Cynthia Fischborn, a graduate home economist with a Bachelor of Science degree from Oregon State University, brings a wealth of experience to her writing. This mother of two young children taught Home Economics in public school for many years and found time to write a newspaper column, edit a microwave magazine and several cookbooks. She has also given classes at cooking schools in the Northwest and has worked with various microwave manufacturers, culinary publications and food commissions, testing and developing recipes for consumers.

Cheryl Long majored in Home Economics and Communication at Cal State University, Long Beach, and Marylhurst College in Oregon. Her experience in the microwave industry is impressive, acquired while working for many years with Litton Industries and Quasar. There she served as microwave coordinator, trainer for cooking school instructors and Home Economics teachers, with emphasis on business application in the industry. This author of several cookbooks has also been a newspaper and magazine columnist, editor of a microwave magazine, and microwave cooking instructor at the college level. She is the mother of two boys.

This book is lovingly dedicated to our mothers, who gave us our first cooking lessons and, instead of laughing, encouraged us.

Chapter One

INTRODUCTION TO
MICROWAVE PRESERVING

*y*ou might be tempted to skip this factual chapter and get right to the recipes. **Please don't!** We want you to be successful with your microwave preserving recipes, and so in this chapter, we have provided essential information on:

• what utensils to cook in

• how to adjust cooking times to your microwave oven wattage, if necessary

• definitions of microwave power settings

• two basic methods for prolonged food storage

• what you'll need to know about kitchen wraps, high-altitude cooking, metric and equivalent measures.

By taking a few minutes to check this information first, your microwave preserving experience will be knowledgeable, easy and fun — not confusing. Relax, refer to the charts and directions as needed, and make something wonderful!

RECIPE TIMING ADJUSTMENT GUIDE FOR MICROWAVE OVENS

Recipes in this book have been tested in 650 to 700 watt microwave ovens. If your oven falls within this wattage range, use cooking times as given. Microwave ovens with lower wattage require an increase in cooking time, as shown in the guide below:

650 TO 700 WATTS If time is:	500 TO 625 WATTS Add 20%:	400 TO 500 WATTS Add 35%:
30 seconds	35 seconds	45 seconds
1 minute	1 min. 10 sec.	1 min. 25 sec.
2 minutes	2 min. 30 sec.	2 min. 45 sec.
5 minutes	6 minutes	7 minutes
10 minutes	12 minutes	14 minutes
15 minutes	18 minutes	20 minutes
20 minutes	24 minutes	27 minutes
30 minutes	36 minutes	41 minutes

MICROWAVE POWER SETTINGS

Since there are no standards in the microwave industry for power setting terminology, we are including the following chart to explain the terminology used in this book.

HIGH: 100% power
This setting used to be called "COOK". Used for boiling water, liquids and for blanching and cooking fresh and frozen fruits and vegetables.

MEDIUM-HIGH: 70% power
Sometimes call "ROAST". Used for many things, such as maintaining a gentler boiling point or on more delicate mixtures.

MEDIUM: 50% power
Sometimes called "SIMMER". Gives low, gentle heating for finer textured foods and for simmering foods.

DEFROST: 30 - 33% power
Sometimes the same as "LOW". Primary use is to defrost foods. It can also be used to cook delicate foods.

LOW: 20 - 25% power
Sometimes the same as "DEFROST" on some ovens.

WARM: 10% power
This is becoming a common term on most all ovens. Ideal for holding foods warm and very delicate foods.

MICROWAVE COOKING UTENSILS

Using the right utensil can mean the difference between a perfectly prepared recipe or a frustrating cooking experience.

While some of today's microwave ovens are metal-tolerant to some degree, this does not mean that food can be cooked in conventional metal pots and pans. Instead, use glass or Corning casseroles and lids, glass mixing bowls, or glass measuring cups, including the extra-large two-quart "batter" bowl. Rigid microwave-safe thermoplastic containers (these should be clearly labeled "for microwave use") are also usable. But do avoid using softer plastics; they cannot take the heat from the hot food and can melt, sag, etc.. Most of all, remember to make sure that all of your microwave containers are deep enough to prevent boil-overs.

Do not leave metal spoons or conventional thermometers in preserving containers while the oven is operating. Wooden spoons may, if desired, be left in while the oven is operating; however, the moisture will warm the spoon if it is left in for a long period of time. Microwave-safe thermometers or probes may, of course, be left in the container while micro-cooking.

USE OF KITCHEN WRAPS IN MICROWAVE PRESERVING

PLASTIC WRAP: Most preferred and versatile wrap used in microwave cooking. When recipe directions say "cover", plastic wrap may be used in place of a lid. Remember that plastic wrap will trap and hold in all of the steam; it is not porous. Therefore it is necessary to allow some of the steam to escape, so that the plastic wrap will not bulge or lie flat on the food. There are two ways to do this:

1. Lift a small (1″) section of the plastic wrap at the edge or corner of the bowl or container, or

2. Using a toothpick, put several holes in the center of the plastic after sealing to the edges of the container.

Note: When removing plastic wrap, be careful to lift the edge farthest away from you, pulling plastic wrap towards you. This allows the hot steam to escape away from you into the air. Remember **hot steam can burn!**

WAXED PAPER: Is semi-porous and may be used as a lid or covering for foods needing some moisture held in, but not to the point of steaming. Good as a splatter shield where a tight-fitting cover is not necessary.

PAPER TOWELS AND NAPKINS: Are very porous, which allows steam to pass through while absorbing some excess moisture. Although excellent for reheating bread products, these are not a good choice as a covering for recipes in this book. And remember **do not use towels made from recycled paper**; they may contain impurities such as metal particles, which could heat and ignite the paper.

ALUMINIUM FOIL: Since metal reflects microwaves, (and prevents cooking), aluminium foil wrap is **not** a suitable covering for cooking foods.

BOILING WATER BATH PROCESS

This conventional method of processing is recommended for canning fruits, jams, jellies, pickled vegetables and tomatoes where a long shelf-life is desired. It is not necessary for shorter term refrigeration or, of course, freezing.

Bring water to a boil conventionally in a water bath canner. Immerse filled, sealed jars into boiling water. Water level should be one inch or more above the top of the jars. Start counting the processing time as soon as all jars have been added and water returns to a boil. Boil gently and steadily for time recommended. Higher altitudes, over 1,000 feet, require longer processing times (see chart below).

For further information or questions about conventional boiling water bath processing, contact your local USDA Extension office.

BOILING WATER BATH HIGH-ALTITUDE CHART

Additional Processing Times

Altitude	Less than 20 minutes	More than 20 minutes
1,000 feet	2 minutes	3 minutes
2,000 feet	3 minutes	4 minutes
3,000 feet	3 minutes	6 minutes
4,000 feet	4 minutes	8 minutes
5,000 feet	5 minutes	10 minutes
6,000 feet	6 minutes	12 minutes
7,000 feet	7 minutes	14 minutes
8,000 feet	8 minutes	16 minutes
9,000 feet	9 minutes	18 minutes
10,000 feet	10 minutes	20 minutes

EQUIVALENT MEASURES

Dash	=			2 to 4 drops
3 teaspoons	=	1 tablespoon	=	½ fluid ounce
4 tablespoons	=	¼ cup	=	2 fluid ounces
16 tablespoons	=	1 cup (½ pint)	=	8 fluid ounces
2 cups	=	1 pint	=	16 fluid ounces
2 pints	=	1 quart	=	32 fluid ounces
4 quarts	=	1 gallon	=	128 fluid ounces
2 tablespoons	=	⅛ cup	=	1 ounce
4 tablespoons	=	¼ cup	=	2 ounces
16 tablespoons	=	1 cup	=	8 ounces
2 cups	=	1 pound	=	16 ounces

METRIC CONVERSION

1 milliliter	=	.034 fluid ounces
1 liter	=	33.8 fluid ounces or 4.2 cups
1 fluid ounce	=	29.56 milliliters
1 fluid cup	=	236 milliliters
1 fluid quart	=	946 milliliters or .946 liters
1 teaspoon	=	5 milliliters
tablespoon	=	15 milliliters

BLANCHING ALMONDS

Measure 1 cup hot tap water in a 4-cup glass measure. Microwave on HIGH (100%) power for 1-1/2 minutes, or until water comes to a boil. Add 1 cup shelled, unblanched almonds. Microwave mixture for 1 minute on HIGH (100%) power. Drain and place on paper toweling to cool slightly. Rub with hands or toweling, skins will slip off.

Chapter Two

FRUIT AND VEGETABLE

BASICS

FRUIT AND VEGETABLE BASICS

This chapter has some of the more important preserving information contained in the book. It includes such vital items as blanching charts, syrup tables, freezing facts as well as sugar alternatives in preserving and more. Read this chapter before you begin for a basic understanding of the techniques used in microwave preserving.

Freezing fresh fruits in a sugar-syrup allows great versatility and ease in menu planning. These fresh flavored fruits with a sparkling of sweetness may be used for compotes, pies, cobblers, ice cream toppings, or served as is. Refer to the **Defrosting Frozen Fruit Chart** if speed is of the essence.

If you are fortunate enough to have your own backyard garden or access to fresh-picked vegetables, the microwave oven will be your best preserving friend. The microwave oven is ideal for blanching fresh-picked vegetables. When blanching large quantities of vegetables, we recommend an assembly-line approach. Process 1 to 2 pounds at a time in the microwave oven while preparing the next batch. (See blanching chart for complete details.) We find this method is cool, easy, efficient and it produces superior fresh-tasting vegetables.

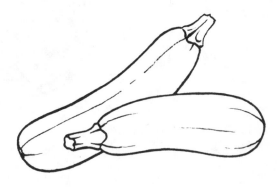

DEFROSTING FROZEN FRUIT

Amount	Defrosting Time at 30% power
10-oz. carton/container	3-4 minutes
1 pt. container	5 to 6 minutes
1 qt. container	9 to 10 minutes

Let container rest for 5 to 10 minutes after microwaving to complete defrosting. Increase time for larger containers.

FRUIT FREEZING FACTS

Most fruits freeze very well. If properly prepared: they will retain bright, natural color, flavor and nutritive value. Some guidelines to follow are:

- Select fresh, ripe fruit just as you would for eating.
- Wash the fruit gently in cold water; drain well.
- Decide on method desired for freezing: in sugar syrup, unsweetened pack or sugar pack.
- Prepare fruit for freezing and pack into appropriate freezer containers. Allow ½″ headspace for dry or sugar packed fruits. Allow 1″ headspace for all liquid or syrup packs.
- Floating fruits that tend to darken can be kept below the surface of the liquid by crumpling waxed paper, parchment or plastic wrap atop fruit in container before sealing. These papers are not affected by microwave defrosting.
- Seal, label and date containers. Freeze quickly at 0° F. or below. Frozen fruits may be stored 8 to 12 months. Do not refreeze thawed fruits.

FROZEN FRUIT YIELD

To obtain 1 pint of frozen fruit, follow quantities listed below.

FRUIT	AMOUNT
Apples	1¼ to 1½ lbs.
Apricots	⅔ to ¾ lb.
Berries, small*	1⅓ to 1½ pint
Berries, large**	1 pint
Cherries	1 lb.
Peaches/Nectarines	1 to 1½ lbs.
Pears	1 to 1¼ lbs.
Rhubarb	⅔ to 1 lb.
Strawberries	⅔ qt.

* Such as blackberries, blueberries, elderberries, gooseberries, huckleberries, etc.

** Such as boysenberries, loganberries, marionberries, raspberries, etc.

UNSWEETENED FRUIT PACK

Some fruits, such as blueberries, don't require added sugar or liquids for proper freezing. This is commonly called a "dry" pack.

Other fruits, such as apples and peaches, will darken if not treated before freezing. If you choose not to use sugar or sugar syrup, you may substitute a solution of water and ascorbic acid color keeper. Add ¾ teaspoon ascorbic acid color keeper to each quart of water. Place prepared fruit in freezer container. Pour enough ascorbic acid/water solution over fruit to cover, leaving adequate headspace. A good way to prevent floating fruit, which will darken, is to put crumpled wax, parchment or other water-resistant paper in this headspace before sealing. Fruit prepared in this manner, often called a "wet" pack, may be used later for microwave jams and jellies if desired, as well as other recipes, etc.

SUGAR SYRUPS

Making sugar syrups in the microwave oven is a fast shortcut when canning fruits. Use your larger glass measuring cups or a 2-quart microwave batter bowl to prepare sugar syrups. These will not only measure the ingredients but also serve as excellent containers for microwave cooking. Since they also have a pour spout, it is much easier to fill jars or freezer containers by pouring, rather than by the often-messy ladling method.

Type of Syrup	Sugar (Cups)	Water (Cups)	Minutes at HIGH power	Yield (Cups)
LIGHT	1	4	12	5
THIN	2	4	13	5
MEDIUM	3	4	14	5½
HEAVY	4¾	4	16	6½
VERY HEAVY	7	4	18	7¾

In a 2-quart batter bowl or large mixing bowl, combine sugar and water according to chart; stir to mix well. Microwave as directed until mixture boils, stirring once halfway through cooking time. Remove and stir, making sure sugar is completely dissolved.

• For canning: Pour hot sugar syrup into prepared jars full of fruit. If you need to keep the syrup hot until jars are ready, hold syrup on WARM (10%) power setting until needed. (If more than 60 minutes, it may be simpler to reheat syrup.)

• For Freezing: Let cool to room temperature, covered. Chill in refrigerator. Be sure syrup is well chilled before pouring over fruit in freezer containers.

TIP: To Make Ahead: Syrup may be made the day before and stored in the refrigerator.

TIP: To Prevent Darkened Fruit: If sugar syrup is to be used on a fruit that tends to darken, add ascorbic acid color keeper to sugar syrup after it has cooled. Add ¾ teaspoon ascorbic acid color keeper to each quart of syrup.

ALTERNATIVES TO CANNING WITH SUGAR SYRUPS

Those who wish to reduce the amount of sugar used or to eliminate it altogerther may wonder how this may be done and what to substitute. We have used the following substitutions successfully. Process canned fruits conventionally in a boiling water bath. Preparation processes may be done with the quick help of your microwave oven.

Its easy to use your microwave oven to heat water, fruit juices, or syrups quickly. Microwave on HIGH (100%) power until warmed to desired temperature or just until liquid comes to a boil. If heating syrups in their glass container remember to remove lid first. Syrup at narrow neck will be hotter than the rest of the bottle. Handle carefully; hot pads may be in order.

1. Pack fruit in plain hot water. You may wish to add ascorbic acid to prevent darkening, if appropriate.

2. Pack fruit in hot fruit juice. (Pineapple or pear juice is very sweet if fruit is tart, or use the same type of juice as fruit being preserved.)

3. Place 1 to 2 tablespoons of honey or pure maple syrup on top of fruit packed in jar and pour boiling water over before sealing jar for processing.

4. Add one or more of the following to each jar of fruit: one slice of lemon, 1 clove, stick of cinnamon.

5. Make a syrup using honey or pure maple syrup and hot water to pack fruit.

SELECTING VEGETABLES FOR FREEZING

The best vegetables for freezing probably come from your own backyard garden. However, fresh produce can also be found at roadside stands, U-pick farms, or even a market with an excellent produce section. Whatever your choice, select the freshest possible produce and prepare for freezing immediately or refrigerate until preparation time. Ideally, fresh vegetables should be gathered early in the morning before they have absorbed much heat. If storage is necessary, make sure it is for the shortest time possible in order to obtain peak flavor, quality and food value. Do not select overripe vegetables as they can be tough and flavorless.

WHAT TO LOOK FOR IN A VEGETABLE:

Asparagus:
Young, tender stalks; crisp; with well-formed tightly closed tips; about 2-inch light-colored woody base.

Beans, green:
Young, tender, crisp snap; with long, straight pods.

Broccoli:
Firm, tender stalks; with tight, compact, dark green heads, not woody.

Brussels Sprouts:
Firm, compact, bright green heads; small to medium sized heads.

Carrots:
Firm, well-shaped, bright color, mild-flavored, not excessively large, woody or shriveled.

Cauliflower:
Firm, tender, snow-white head, heavy compact head with a bright green covering of leaves.

Celery:
Firm, compact stalk, not pithy or stringy. Should be brittle enough to snap easily. Avoid stalks with brown spots or seed formation in center.

Corn:
Young, tender, even rows of plump, milky kernels with a fresh green husk.

Onions, tiny white:
Bright, clean, firm and well-shaped with dry skins. Avoid onions that have sprouted at the neck or have soft spots.

Parsnips:
Firm, medium-sized, well-shaped and smooth; avoid soft, very large or limp parsnips.

Peas:
Bright green, well-filled pods; plump peas.

Pea Pods:
Bright green, slightly velvety, fresh-picked; avoid limp, discolored, wet or mildewed pods.

Rutabagas:
Roots heavy for size, firm, smooth, small to medium in size.

Spinach:
Young, tender leaves, crisp, not limp leaves.

Squash, summer:
Young, with small seeds and firm, tender rind; heavy for size, glossy.

Squash, winter:
Mature, fully colored, firm, hard rind; heavy for size.

Swiss Chard:
Bright white or red stalks, young tender leaves; crisp, not limp, leaves.

Turnips:
Heavy for size, firm, smooth, fairly round, small to medium in size.

FROZEN VEGETABLE YIELD

In general, the following amount of vegetable as purchased will yield one pint frozen:

Vegetable	Pounds

Asparagus . . . . 1 to 1½
Beans, green . . . . ⅔ to 1
Broccoli 1
Brussels Sprouts 1
Carrots, without tops . . . . 1¼ to 1½
Cauliflower 1⅓
Celery . . . . 1 to 1¼
Corn, on the cob, in husks . . . . 2 to 2½
Onions, whole, tiny 1
Parsnips 1¼
Peas . . . . 2 to 2½
Peapods 1
Rutabagas . . . . ⅔
Spinach . . . . 1 to 1½
Squash, summer . . . . 1 to 1¼
Squash, winter 1½
Swiss Chard . . . . 1 to 1¼
Turnips . . . . ⅔

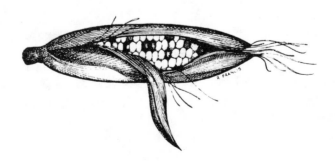

COOKING FROZEN VEGETABLES IN YOUR MICROWAVE

There are basically two ways to properly cook frozen vegetables in your microwave oven. Vegetables frozen in heat-sealed plastic bags* may be left in the bag for cooking, while vegetables frozen in rigid types of freezer containers must be removed and placed in a microwave-safe utensil for cooking.

With either method, it is not necessary to thaw or defrost vegetables or add any large quantities of additional water. If water is added, a tablespoon or two is usually sufficient. Microwaved vegetables cook quickly, (6 to 7 minutes per lb.).

*Note: Do not use regular or freezer plastic bags to cook vegetables in the microwave oven. Even heavy-duty freezer bags will melt at low temperatures (140° to 180°F).

VEGETABLES IN A HEAT-SEALED PLASTIC BAG

1 pint or 10 oz. frozen vegetables

Place bag on microwave-safe plate or bowl. Cut a ½″ slit on the top side of the bag.

• For tender-crisp vegetables: Microwave on HIGH (100% power) for 4 to 6 minutes. Quarter-turn dish halfway through cooking time if necessary. Let rest in container for 4 to 5 minutes. Check vegetables for desired doneness. Serve.

• For softer, less crisp vegetables: Microwave on HIGH (100% power) for 5 to 8 minutes. Quarter-turn dish halfway through cooking time if necessary. Let rest in container 5 to 10 minutes. Check vegetables for desired doneness. Serve.

Tip: Cooking time on vegetables will vary depending upon the type of vegetable being cooked; for example, petite peas take minimum time and lima beans take maximum time.

24

VEGETABLE BLANCHING CHART

BASIC DIRECTIONS: Prepare vegetable as indicated. Place vegetable in microwave container; cover with lid or plastic wrap. Microwave on HIGH (100%) power for all blanching times shown. After blanching, drain vegetable in colander. Plunge colander containing vegetable into ice water for several minutes. Drain, then pack into freezer container, seal, label, date and freeze.

Asparagus:
2 cups (1 lb.) Wash. Trim off white woody end. Cut to container length or 2″ pieces. For long stalks, alternate top and bottom ends when placing in blanching container. Add ¼ cup water; cover. Rearrange or stir halfway through cooking. Chill, pack and freeze. Blanching time: 3 minutes.

Green Beans:
3 cups (1 lb.) Wash; remove ends. Cut into 1 or 2″ pieces or French cut. Add ½ cup water; cover. Stir halfway through cooking. Chill, pack and freeze. Blanching time: 4 minutes.

Broccoli:
3 cups (1½ lbs.) Wash; trim base stalk; peel large end of stalk if desired. Split lengthwise into 1″ stalks. For chopped broccoli, cut into ½″ pieces after trimming. Add ½ cup water, cover. Rearrange or stir halfway through cooking. Chill, pack and freeze. Blanching time: 5 minutes.

Brussels Sprouts:
4 cups (1 lb.) Cut from stem; wash well. Remove imperfect outer leaves. Note: If precut from stem at purchase, trim base. Add ¼ cup water, cover. Stir once halfway through cooking. Chill, pack and freeze. Blanching time: 4½ minutes.

Carrots:
4 cups (1¼ lbs.) Wash; scrape or peel. Cut into ¼ inch slices. Add ½ cup water; cover. Stir once halfway through cooking. Chill, pack and freeze. Blanching time: 5 minutes.

Cauliflower:
1 head (1 lb.) Wash; trim woody base and cut into small flowerettes or 1″ pieces. Add ½ cup water; cover. Stir halfway through cooking. Chill, pack and freeze. Blanching time: 3½ minutes.

Celery:
4 cups (1 lb.) Wash; trim base and leafy tops. Cut into ½″ slices, tops optional. Add ⅛ cup water, cover. Stir once halfway through cooking. Chill, pack and freeze. Blanching time: 6 minutes.

Corn, Kernel:
2 cups, Husk; remove silk and wash. Cut corn kernels off (whole or cream style) and place in blanching container. Add ⅛ cup water, cover. Stir once halfway through cooking. Chill, pack and freeze. Blanching time: 3 minutes.

Corn, On The Cob (In Husk):
4 ears, May be prepared and frozen in husk. Trim both ends of excess silks and stem. Remove excessive outer husk. Rinse and shake to partly dry. Note: For long term (over 3 months) freezer storage we recommend removing corn kernels from cob before blanching as above. Arrange ears with 1″ air space on all sides. Rearrange halfway through cooking. Chill, pack and freeze. Blanching time: 4 minutes.

Corn, On The Cob (Out of Husk):
4 ears, Husk, remove silk, wash and trim off excess stem. Add ¼ cup water; cover. Rearrange halfway through cooking. Chill, pack and freeze. Blanching time: 4½ minutes.

Onions, Chopped:
4½ cups (1¼ lbs.) Trim both ends; slit outer skin from top to bottom. Peel away outer layer. Rinse, chop. Add ¼ cup water; cover. Stir halfway through cooking. Chill, pack and freeze. Blanching time: 3½ minutes.

Onions, Whole, Tiny:
2 cups (¾ lb.) Trim both ends; slit outer skin from top to bottom. Peel off out layer; rinse. Add ¼ cup water, cover. Stir halfway through cooking. Chill, pack and freeze. Blanching time: 3 minutes.

Parsnips:
Scant 2 cups (⅔ lb.) Wash and peel. Trim ends and cut into ½" cubes. Add ¼ cup water; cover. Stir halfway through cooking. Chill, pack and freeze. Blanching time: 3 minutes.

Peas:
2 cups (2 lbs.) Shell, discard imperfect peas. Add ¼ cup water; cover. Stir halfway through cooking. Chill, pack and freeze. Blanching time: 3½ minutes.

Pea Pods:
2 cups (1 lb.) Snap off ends and remove strings. Rinse. Add ⅛ cup water; cover. Stir halfway through cooking. Chill, pack and freeze. Blanching time: 2 minutes.

Rutabagas:
4 cups (1¼ lbs.) Wash, cut off tops, peel, cut into ½" cubes. Add ½ cup water; cover. Stir halfway through cooking. Chill, pack and freeze. Blanching time: 5 minutes.

Spinach:
12 cups (1 lb.) Wash well, soak in cold water 5 minutes. Rinse with cold water. Cut and discard thick stem ends and any imperfect leaves. Add ⅛ cup water; cover. Stir halfway through cooking. Chill, pack and freeze. Blanching time: 3 to 3½ minutes.

Squash, Summer (All Varieties):
(1 lb.) Wash; trim both ends. Cut into ½" slices or chunks. Add ¼ cup water; cover. Stir halfway through cooking. Chill, pack and freeze. Blanching time: 2½ to 4 minutes.

Swiss Chard:
10 cups (1 lb.) Wash well. Trim any imperfect leaves and stem ends. Cut into 1" pieces. Add ⅛ cup water; cover. Stir halfway through cooking. Chill, pack and freeze. Blanching time: 3 to 3½ minutes.

Turnips:
3 cups (¾ lb.) Wash, cut off tops, peel, cut into ½" cubes. Add ¼ cup water; cover. Stir halfway through cooking. Chill, pack and freeze. Blanching time: 3 minutes.

REHYDRATING DRIED VEGETABLES

To rehydrate dried vegetables conveniently, just place them in a microwave-safe bowl. Pour cold water over vegetables and stir once gently to make sure vegetables are immersed in water. Cover bowl with microwave-safe cover or plastic wrap. Microwave on HIGH (100%) power just to the boiling point. Leave cover in place, set aside and let rest until vegetables are completely rehydrated.

Chapter Three

FRUITS AND
FRUIT SAUCES

FRUITS AND FRUIT SAUCES

This chapter is a potpourri of fruits and fruit sauces, all so simply made in your microwave oven. We have found that fruits are an absolute natural in the microwave: they require little cooking due to their delicate nature. You'll find family favorites such as **Chunky Applesauce** and **Cranberry Sauce** as well as such unique and gourmet delights as **Zucchini Applesauce** and **Wild Blackberry Topping with Liqueur.**

One question we are often asked is, "Can you dry fruit leathers in your microwave oven?" The answer is, "Not well." The microwave oven is a moist-cooking appliance and, as such, it doesn't *dry* exceptionally well.

Drying fruit leathers is best done in a food dryer, especially where large quantities are desired. The microwave oven can, however, assist this process by quickly and easily preheating and precooking the puréed fruit. This eliminates the *browning* which occurs with some fruits. It also makes the use of preservatives unnecessary and will speed up the drying process.

MICROWAVE AND FOOD DRYER PREPARATION OF FRUIT LEATHER

Especially good for apricot, apple, peach and pear fruit leathers but can be used with most fruits and berries. Quantity: 2½ cups fruit purée makes one 18" × 14" × ⅛" sheet of fruit leather.

Puréed fruit of choice

Place puréed fruit in microwave 2-quart batter bowl or larger mixing bowl, as appropriate to quantity. Cover with plastic wrap and microwave on HIGH (100%) power just to the boiling point. Stir occasionally. (Stop when tiny bubbles appear around the edges of the bowl.) **Do not let boil.**

Pour heated purée onto food dryer trays designed for fruit leathers. Dry in food dryer at 130° to 135°F until dry (about 8 hours).

CHUNKY APPLESAUCE

A versatile recipe that can be coarsely chopped, finely chopped or blended to produce the texture preferred. Tastes wonderfully old-fashioned but quick and simple to make. Makes about 3 pints.

6 cups peeled, seeded and coarsely chunked or chopped
    apples, (about 8 apples)
¼ cup water
½ to ¾ cup granulated sugar
½ to 1 tsp. ground cinnamon, optional

In a deep 3-quart or larger bowl combine apples, water and cinnamon. Cover bowl with plastic wrap, lifting one corner up for a steam vent. Microwave on HIGH (100%) power for 4 minutes. Stir, recover and microwave for 4 minutes more. Stir in sugar. Microwave 2 minutes on HIGH (100%) power. Let stand, covered for 5 to 10 minutes. Place in desired containers.

• For immediate use: Refrigerate up to 2 weeks.

• For longer storage: Freeze; leave 1-inch headspace.

•To can: Pack into jars while hot. Process sealed jars conventionally in a boiling water bath canner for 15 minutes.

Variations:
TRADITIONAL APPLESAUCE: Cook as directed. Stir and mash cooked apples to consistency desired. Food processor or blender may be used.
CHUNKY PEARSAUCE: Substitute pears for apples, omitting water. Cook and store as directed for applesauce.
For **SMOOTH PEARSAUCE** follow **TRADITIONAL APPLESAUCE** directions.

ZUCCHINI APPLESAUCE

Tastes just like applesauce. What a sneaky way to use up that excess zucchini! Makes 2½ cups.

¼ cup water
¼ tsp. salt, optional
2 whole cloves
2 thin lemon slices
2 cups peeled and chopped zucchini (apx. 2 medium)
2 cups peeled, cored and chopped apples (apx. 2 apples)
½ cup granulated sugar
½ tsp. ground cinnamon
1 Tbsp. lemon juice

In a large mixing bowl; combine water, salt, cloves and lemon slices. Stir and microwave on HIGH (100%) power for 1 minute or to a boil. Stir in zucchini and apples, cover bowl with plastic wrap and microwave on HIGH for 6 minutes, or until tender, stirring once halfway through cooking. Remove cloves and lemon slices. Pour into blender or food processor and process until desired texture is reached (this goes very quickly).

Pour back into mixing bowl and stir in sugar, cinnamon and lemon juice. Pour into desired container(s). Serve at room temperature or chilled.

• For immediate use: refrigerate up to 2 weeks.

• For longer storage: freeze; leave 1-inch headspace.

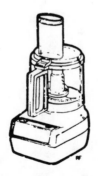

BASIC CRANBERRY SAUCE

Microwave cranberry sauce is amazingly easy to make and delightfully fresh-tasting. Makes 1 quart.

1 lb. fresh **or** frozen cranberries, (about 3½ cups)
1 cup sugar
⅓ cup water

In a 3-quart bowl or casserole, combine ingredients; mix well. Microwave covered, on HIGH (100%) power 6 minutes, stirring once, halfway through cooking time. Check for doneness; cranberry skins should have popped. If not, continue cooking for 1 to 2 minutes more. Let rest covered for 10 minutes.

Refrigerate for short-term use or pack and freeze, leaving ½-inch headspace in container.

Variation: CRANBERRY-ORANGE SAUCE: Substitute orange juice for water and add 1 tablespoon fresh grated orange peel. Optional: Add ¼ cup chopped walnuts after cooking.

CRANBERRY JEWELS IN LIQUEUR

This elegant and colorful sauce is perfect for gifting and special meals. The recipe is from **HOW TO MAKE DANISH FRUIT LIQUEURS** *by Cheryl Long. Makes about 3 cups.*

2 cups cranberries, fresh **or** frozen
1 cup sugar
½ cup orange juice
1 can (11 oz.) Mandarin oranges, well drained
¼ cup orange liqueur

In a 1½ to 2-quart casserole or bowl, combine cranberries, sugar and orange juice. Cover and microwave on HIGH (100%) power for 3 minutes. Stir and microwave for 2 to 3 minutes more, or until cranberries have popped their skins. Let stand covered, for 5 minutes. Gently stir in liqueur and drained Mandarin Orange sections. Refrigerate, covered, overnight before serving. Keeps in the refrigerator for one week.

RHUBARB SAUCE

This versatile sauce makes a quick fruit dish topped with cream. It is also an excellent cobbler base. Makes 1 quart.

4 cups sliced fresh rhubarb stalks*
3 Tbsp. water
1 cup sugar

In a 3-quart bowl, combine rhubarb and water; cover. Microwave for 6 minutes on HIGH (100%) power, stirring once halfway through cooking time. Stir in sugar and microwave covered 1½ minutes more on HIGH to dissolve sugar; stir again. Cool. Serve warm or chilled.

• For immediate use: Place in covered container and refrigerate up to 1 week.

• For longer storage: Pack into freezer containers, leaving 1-inch headspace; freeze.

• To can; Pour hot sauce into hot, sterile jars, leaving ½-inch headspace. Seal and process in a conventional boiling water bath canner for 15 minutes (half-pints or pints).

*Note: Frozen rhubarb may be substituted for fresh in this recipe; however, do not add water.

EASY BERRY SAUCE

Whip up this quick and easy sauce using blackberries, blueberries, raspberries, or strawberries. Serve over ice cream, pound cake, or use to make a plain cheesecake spectacular. Makes about 1 pint.

2⅓ cups fresh **or** frozen berries
⅓ cup granulated sugar **or** honey **or** pure maple syrup
1 Tbsp. cornstarch
¼ cup water (omit if using honey or maple syrup)
1 Tbsp. lemon juice
2 Tbsp. lemon, orange **or** blueberry liqueur, optional

Mash ⅓ cup berries with fork, set remaining berries aside. Combine mashed berries with remaining ingredients, except reserved berries, in a 4-cup or larger glass measure. Microwave on HIGH (100%) power for 1 minute, stir. Microwave for 1 to 2 minutes more or until thickened. Stir in reserved berries. Chill until ready to serve. Keeps in refrigerator for several days.

RASPBERRY DESSERT SAUCE

This sauce is a natural. It's fresh tasting, colorful, low-sugar, and makes a plain dessert look spectacular. Try it over cheesecake or pound cake to start. Create "designer" desserts by pouring the sauce onto a dessert plate and arranging fruits, meringue, ice cream, etc. on top. Use your imagination! Makes about 3 cups.

1¼ lbs. fresh raspberries **or** 2 (10-oz.) packages frozen unsweetened raspberries, thawed
¼ to ⅓ cup granulated sugar, to taste
1 Tbsp. kirsch

Wash fresh berries in cool water, drain well. Push berries through a fine sieve placed over a medium mixing bowl. Discard berry pulp. Add sugar to raspberry juice. Microwave on HIGH (100%) power for 2 to 3 minutes, stirring once halfway through. Remove, stir again making sure sugar is well dissolved. Stir in kirsch. Serve chilled.

• For immediate use: Let cool and refrigerate. Keeps several days.

• For longer storage: Prepare as directed but do not add kirsch. Pour into freezer container(s) when cooled slightly, leaving ½" headspace, cover, label and freeze. When ready to use, defrost in microwave on DEFROST (30%) power until liquid but not hot, stir in kirsch. Serve or refrigerate for serving later.

WILD BLACKBERRY TOPPING WITH LIQUEUR

This elegant sauce is surprisingly easy to make. It is a superb topping for ice cream, pound cake, cheesecake or layered in a trifle. What a perfect liqueur-lover's gift! Makes 3 half-pint jars.

4 cups blackberries, washed and drained
2 cups granulated sugar
¼ cup lemon **or** orange liqueur

Place washed berries in a large 3-quart or larger bowl. Crush slightly. Microwave on HIGH (100%) power for 5 minutes. Stir in sugar and microwave on MEDIUM-HIGH (70%) power for 20 minutes, stirring every 5 minutes. Remove from microwave oven and let cool for 5 minutes, then stir in liqueur. Ladle into sterile jars, seal and label.

• For immediate use: Place in covered container and refrigerate up to 3 weeks.

• To can; Ladle into hot, sterile jars, leaving 1/2-inch headspace. Seal and process conventionally in a boiling water canner for 5 minutes.

PLUMPING DRIED FRUITS

For moist and plump dried fruits place dried fruits in a glass measuring cup or bowl and cover with warm tap water or other liquid.* Microwave on HIGH (100%) power just until liquid comes to a boil. Let rest 5 to 10 minutes.

*Note: 1 cup each of raisins and water take about 3 to 4 minutes. This method also works if fruit juice, wine, rum, sherry brandy or liqueurs are substituted for the water. These are unique and tasty variations for special cakes, fruitcakes, puddings, etc.

SPICED CRAB APPLES

Old-fashioned spiced crab apples are easy to make in your microwave oven. Extra special served with roast pork. Makes about 5 pints.

2½ lbs. crab apples
3 cups granulated sugar
1 cup white **or** cider vinegar
1 cup water
2 cinnamon sticks, broken in half
1 tsp. whole cloves
6 to 8 drops red food coloring, optional

Rinse crab apples; remove and discard stems. Set apples aside. Prepare syrup in a deep 4-quart or larger glass bowl by combining sugar, vinegar, water and spices. Stir to mix well. Microwave on HIGH (100%) power 10 to 12 minutes or until mixture comes to a boil, stirring once halfway through cooking time. Add crab apples, stirring gently and microwave on HIGH power until mixture just returns to a boil. Reduce to MEDIUM (50 to 70%) power and simmer mixture for about 10 to 12 minutes or until crab apples are tender. Stir gently occasionally.

Remove from microwave oven. Use a slotted spoon to remove crab apples from syrup and loosely pack apples into hot, sterile pint jars, leaving a one-half inch headspace. (Do not overpack apples as they will lose their shape.) Return bowl with pickling syrup to microwave oven and bring back to a boil on HIGH power. Remove and stir in food coloring, if desired. Pour over apples up to one-half inch headspace. Wipe rims and seal. Process sealed jars conventionally in a boiling water bath canner for 20 minutes; start timing when water comes to a boil.

Tip: Do not use ground cinnamon as it causes syrup to boil over.

FROZEN MELON BALL MIX

Freezer fresh melon balls can be frozen to enjoy all year long. Serve for breakfast, brunch, appetizer or dessert. Serve partially thawed as is or with a little ginger ale poured over. Makes about 6 pints.

2 cups granulated sugar
4 cups water
½ cup orange juice concentrate
½ cup lemonade concentrate
8 cups assorted melon balls (Persian, watermelon, cantaloupe, honeydew, casaba, etc.)
1 cup blueberries

In a 2-quart batter bowl, combine sugar and water, stir. Microwave on HIGH (100%) power for 6 to 8 minutes, or until mixture comes to a boil, stirring twice. Remove and stir, making sure sugar is completely dissolved. Add lemonade and orange juice concentrates to hot sugar syrup, mixing well. Let cool while packing fruit into freezer containers. Pour cooled syrup over melon balls, leaving ½" headspace. Seal and freeze.

DRIED CITRUS PEEL

Fresh-tasting dried citrus peel is quick, easy and economical to make in your microwave oven.

1 orange **or**
2 lemons **or**
3 limes
waxed paper

Finely grate peel onto square of waxed paper. Microwave on HIGH (100%) power for 2 to 2½ minutes, rearranging every minute. Let cool. Test for dryness. Place dried peel in a tightly sealed jar. Store at room temperature or freeze for longer storage.

OLD-FASHIONED BRANDIED FRUIT

*This recipe updates an old, time-consuming favorite —
brandied fruit. Apricots, cherries, seedless grapes,
kumquats, peaches, pineapple or plums may be used
singly or in any combination you desire. Serve over ice
cream, pound cake, cheesecake or any other creative
dessert your imagination can envision. Also excellent
with ham. Makes about 3 pints.*

1½ cups granulated sugar
½ cup water
3½ lbs. firm, ripe fruit
¾ cup brandy

Prepare fruit, wash, pit, cut, de-stem, etc. as
appropriate. Treat fruit to prevent darkening, if desired
(see page 18). Let fruit drain, set aside.

Make syrup by combining sugar and water in a 4-cup or
larger glass measure. Stir and microwave on HIGH
(100%) power for 2 minutes or until it comes to a boil.
Stir and cook 1 to 2 minutes longer or until all sugar is
dissolved. Keep sugar syrup hot on lowest microwave
power setting.

Pack drained fruit into hot, sterilized jars, filling to
within one inch of top. Add brandy to reserved sugar
syrup, stirring to combine. Divide syrup evenly between
jars, filling to within ½ inch of top. Seal.

• For immediate use: Let cool, refrigerate. Keeps 1
month or more.

• For longer storage: Process sealed jars conventionally
in a boiling water bath for 20 minutes. Cool and store.

Chapter Four

JAMS, JELLIES
AND MORE

JAMS, JELLIES AND MORE

Microwave jam and jelly making is our favorite preserving technique. It allows small-batch preparation, which fits into our busy schedules. In addition, we know our preserves won't scorch and do not require constant attention. Boil-overs are a thing of the past as long as a large, deep bowl is used. Be sure to read our **Jam And Jelly Tips** before making your first batch.

Either liquid or powdered pectin may be used in microwave jam and jelly making. It is best, however, not to substitute one for another in a given recipe. The key to understanding the use of these two pectins is to remember that powdered pectin is boiled with the fruit so it dissolves before adding sugar, while liquid pectin is already dissolved and can be added with sugar.

We have found that a homemade jar of preserves is a welcome and treasured gift year-round. Your gourmet friends might especially appreciate our **Pomegranate Jelly**, **Jalapeño Jelly** or **English Lemon Curd**.

JAM AND JELLY TIPS

1. **Do not** double the recipe.
2. **Do not** reduce sugar.
3. For jam and jelly making, be sure to use deep 4-quart or larger glass or microwave-safe bowls.
4. All cooking times given are a guide. You may need to add or subtract cooking time due to brand differences or wattage differences in microwave ovens. Remember to use the highest power setting, 100%. After jam or jelly mixture has come to a full rolling boil, power may be reduced to 50 to 70% for a gentler boil if needed.
5. Wait until the jam or jelly mixture comes to a full rolling boil as the recipe directs. Be patient!
6. Jams and jellies need to be stirred to distribute heat. Frequently jam or jelly mixtures will boil up when stirred — be careful!
7. Sugar mixtures get very hot so remember to use pot holders when removing bowls from the microwave oven.
8. Whenever pectin is added, add it gradually, stirring very well.

9. Do not attempt to melt paraffin in your microwave oven. Paraffin will not melt under microwave energy. The USDA no longer recommends paraffin sealing.

10. To test jelly for doneness: Dip a metal spoon into boiling jelly, remove and allow the juice to drip from the side of the spoon. As it nears the jelly stage it will drip from the spoon in two drops, ¼ to ½ inch apart; when the jellying point has been reached the two drops will run together and drop off in one sheet or flake.

Appearance of jelly nearing the jellying point.

Appearance of jelly which has reached the jellying point.

11. A conventional candy or jelly thermometer may be used to test for doneness instead of the jelly test. However, be sure to test with the microwave power off. **Do not** leave the thermometer in the microwave oven with the power on. At sea level, the jellying point is reached at 220° to 222°F. At higher altitudes it is reached at lower temperatures.

12. The U.S. Department of Agriculture recommends storing jams in jars with two-part lids and processing in a boiling water bath. See chart following.

Recommended process time for Jellies and Jam with added pectin in a boiling-water bath canner.

Process Time at Altitudes of:

Style of Pack	Jar Size	0–1,000	1,001–6,000 ft	Above 6,000 ft
Hot	Half-pints	5 min.	10 min.	15 min.

JAM AND JELLY DEFINITIONS

Conserve: a mixture of several fruits, cooked to jamlike consistency, with sugar, often with nuts and raisins.

Fruit Butters: a thick, smooth spread made by cooking pureed fruit pulp with sugar and spices.

Jam: a preserve of whole fruit, slightly crushed, cooked with sugar until thick.

Jelly: a clear, transparent preserve that retains its shape when unmolded. Made by cooking a clear liquid (usually fruit juice) with sugar.

Marmalade: a clear, jellylike preserve with fruit (usually citrus) suspended in small pieces or thin slices.

Preserves: fruits or pieces of fruits, cooked with sugar until tender and plump. The fruit remains whole and the syrup becomes transparent and very thick.

44

ALTERNATIVES TO SUGAR AND PECTIN IN JAMS AND JELLIES

Jams, jellies, preserves and fruit sauces can be made sugar free with great results. Sometimes freezer jams don't set up quite as thick when not using sugar. To compensate for this, increase the amount of pectin, or use other thickeners such as tapioca flour or starch, agar-agar (a natural "gel" from seaweed), arrowroot powder or cornstarch. Or simply increase the cooking time, a technique known as "cooking down" or "jamming".

Jam thickens as it cools. One way to test the consistency of jam while it is cooking is to dip a spoon in the simmering jam to see if it coats the spoon. Use the thickener after the jam has been partially reduced through cooking. If you use tapioca flour as a thickener, combine it with a little cold water before adding to jam.

There are no specific rules to follow when substituting honey for a standard canning recipe. Generally, about half as much honey as sugar works, but often less is required, to one's individual taste. Choose a mild-flavored honey or use pure maple syrup. The maple syrup can be used in smaller quantities because it is so concentrated. We recommend using about half as much maple syrup as honey; in this small quantity, it won't change the taste of the fruit.

DE-CRYSTALLIZING HONEY

To decrystallize honey, just place it in the microwave oven (being sure the container is microwave safe). Insert food probe or microwave-safe food thermometer and microwave on HIGH (100%) power to 120°F. Watch, this goes quickly!

TRADITIONAL BERRY FREEZER JAM

Blackberries, blueberries, boysenberries, gooseberries, huckleberries, loganberries, marionberries, raspberries or strawberries will all work well in this recipe. Makes about 6 half-pints.

4 cups slightly crushed fresh berries*
4 cups granulated sugar
2 Tbsp. lemon juice
3 oz. liquid pectin

Combine berries, sugar and lemon juice in a deep 3-quart or larger bowl. Microwave for 7 minutes on HIGH (100%) power; stir well to combine. Continue cooking 5 to 8 minutes more; stirring once halfway through cooking time. Mixture should come to a full boil.

Remove from microwave and stir in pectin, making sure it is well combined. Let cool 2 to 3 minutes. Fill containers to within 1 inch of the top and seal.

• For immediate use: Refrigerate; keeps several weeks.

• For longer storage: Cool to room temperature, then freeze.

*Note: Frozen berries may be used but cooking time will increase by 4 to 6 minutes. If using frozen berries, defrost in microwave on 30% power. One quart (4 cups) takes 5 to 6 minutes. Let rest for 5 minutes after defrosting.

BERRY LOW-SUGAR FREEZER JAM

Blackberries, blueberries, boysenberries, gooseberries, huckleberries, loganberries, marionberries, raspberries or strawberries will all work well in this recipe. Makes 2 half-pints.

2 cups slightly crushed fresh berries *
1 cup granulated sugar
1 Tbsp. lemon juice
1 Tbsp. powdered pectin

Combine berries and pectin in a large mixing bowl. Microwave on HIGH (100%) power for 5 minutes, stirring once (the mixture should boil). Add the sugar and lemon juice, stir. Microwave on HIGH 7 to 9 minutes more, stirring every few minutes, until mixture comes to a full boil and boils for 1 minute.

• For immediate use: Refrigerate up to 2 weeks.

• For longer storage: Freeze; leave 1 ″ headspace.

*Note: Frozen berries may be used but cooking time will increase by 3 to 4 minutes.

PREVENTING BOIL-OVERS

When microwaving jams, jellies or sauces use a large, deep bowl or casserole. To prevent a boil-over, turn off the power. Remember that boiling will stop immediately when the microwave power is interrupted.

PLUM JELLY

While any kind of plum may be used for this recipe, our favorite is the small Japanese plum. Giftable and gourmet, tangy Japanese Plum Jelly is a rare treat. Makes about 4 half-pints.

Extracting Juice From Plums:

2 lbs. fresh plums
½ cup water

Wash plums, drain well. Place plums in a deep 3-quart or larger bowl. Crush plums; add water. Microwave on HIGH (100%) power 10 to 15 minutes, or until mixture comes to a boil. Stir occasionally. Boil 1 minute on HIGH.

Place colander or sieve over a large bowl. Pour cooled plum mixture into colander. Press out all the juice. Discard pits and pulp. Rinse colander and place jelly bag or muslin cloth inside. Set over a large bowl and pour juice through to strain. Do not press pulp through cloth. Juice may be frozen at this point for later use in jelly making.

Making Jelly:

2 cups plum juice
3½ cups sugar
3 oz. liquid pectin

In a deep 3-quart or larger bowl, thoroughly combine juice and sugar. Microwave on HIGH (100%) power for 5 minutes; stir and continue microwaving on HIGH for 5 to 7 minutes more or until mixture comes to a boil. Stir in pectin and microwave on HIGH for 4 to 6 minutes or until mixture returns to a full boil. Continue microwaving 1 additional minute at a full boil. Skim off any foam. Ladle into hot, sterile jelly jars, seal, and follow boiling water bath canner chart on page 44.

POMEGRANATE JELLY

This rich crimson gourmet jelly makes an elegant gift if you can bear to give it away. Makes about 4 half-pint jars.

5 to 6 large pomegranates
½ cup water
1 Tbsp. lemon juice
3 cups granulated sugar
3 oz. liquid pectin

Wash pomegranates. Trim crown and base, then cut into quarters. Pull back and remove one membrane at a time, exposing clusters of seeds. Gently pull seeds away from white centers. Place all seeds in a bowl. Add ½ cup water. Discard all white membranes, centers and peel. Place bowl of seeds in microwave and cook on HIGH (100%) power for 5 minutes to assist in releasing juice.

Use a food mill or a potato masher to crush seeds and extract juice. If using a potato masher, take a square of waxed paper and poke potato masher handle through the center of the waxed paper. Using waxed paper as a shield, mash seeds with potato masher to release juice. Measure juice, adding a small amount of water, if needed, to make 4 cups. (If there is not enough juice, prepare more, or mix a small amount of water with pulp left in food mill and grind again.) Pour juice through a fine strainer into a large deep 4-quart or larger glass bowl to remove any seeds or large pieces. Add lemon juice and sugar to pomegranate juice and stir to combine.

Microwave on HIGH (100%) power for 8 to 10 minutes, or until mixture comes to a full boil. Stir in liquid pectin. Microwave on HIGH until mixture again comes to a full boil, then time for 1 minute at a full boil. Stir carefully. Skim off any foam with a metal spoon. Pour hot jelly into sterile jars, seal, and follow boiling water bath canner chart on page 44.

JUICE JELLY

This versatile jelly can be made with any of the following: apple juice, grape juice, cranberry or cranapple juice cocktail. Makes about 4 half-pint jars.

2 cups juice
3½ cups sugar
3 oz. liquid pectin

Combine juice and sugar in a deep 4-quart or larger bowl. Stir to mix well. Microwave uncovered on HIGH (100%) power until mixture comes to a full boil, about 12 to 14 minutes. Stir halfway through cooking time. After mixture has come to a full boil, stir in pectin. Microwave on HIGH, bringing mixture back up to a full boil. Time at full boil for 1 minute. Skim off any foam with a metal spoon and pour jelly into hot, sterile jars, seal, and follow boiling water bath canner chart on page 44.

Variations:
MINT JELLY: Prepare jelly with apple juice as directed. After skimming, add ½ teaspoon mint extract or 1 drop mint oil and 6 to 8 drops green food coloring (optional). Stir to mix, then pour into hot, sterile jars and seal.

ROSE GERANIUM JELLY: Add 4 rose geranium leaves to apple juice and sugar before cooking. Prepare as directed, removing leaves before ladling into hot sterile jars.

WINE JELLY

You may use any burgundy, champagne, port, red, rosé, white or blush wine you prefer in this recipe. Wine jellies are good served with beef, pork, lamb or duck. Can also be spread over cream cheese and served with crackers or bread. Makes about 4 half-pint jars.

1 ¾ cups wine
3 cups sugar
3 oz. liquid pectin

In a large, deep mixing bowl, combine wine and sugar. Microwave on HIGH (100%) power for 5 minutes. Stir and continue to microwave until mixture begins to boil (about 4 to 5 minutes more). Time for 1 minute at a full boil. Stir and slowly add pectin, stirring to mix well.

Skim and ladle into hot, sterile jars, seal and follow boiling water bath canner chart on page 44.

Tip: For something elegant try one of these presentations:

- Ladle hot jelly into sterile, stemmed wine glasses. Cover with a small piece of plastic wrap and cool. Use when cooled and set or refrigerate.

- Place a small washed bunch of fresh grapes into hot, sterile custard cups. Ladle hot jelly over grapes. Cover with a small piece of plastic wrap and cool. Use when cooled and set or refrigerate. Do not keep these over one month as grapes will not hold.

1-2-3-ALARM JALAPEÑO JELLY

A colorful hors d'oeuvre served over cream cheese with crackers. This giftable jelly can be any degree of hotness you wish--choose the 'alarm' you want. Makes 4 half-pint jars.

2 large green peppers, washed and seeded
1 jalapeño pepper*, washed and seeded
4 cups granulated sugar
¾ cup white **or** white wine vinegar
3 oz. liquid pectin
3 to 4 drops food coloring, optional

Purée or grind all peppers together. Measure 1½ cups. Mix ground peppers and their juices with sugar and vinegar in a large, deep bowl. Cover with waxed paper, and microwave on HIGH (100% power) for 10 to 12 minutes, stirring halfway through. Remove waxed paper and microwave for 1 to 2 more minutes, bringing to a boil. Add pectin, stir well. Microwave 2 minutes more. Stir in food coloring if desired. Skim and pour into hot, sterile jars, seal and follow boiling water bath canner chart on page 44.

*Note: Adjust hotness of jelly as follows:

　　　1 Alarm (mild): 1 jalapeño pepper
　　　2 Alarm (medium): 2 jalapeño peppers
　　　3 Alarm (hot): 3 jalapeño peppers

Variation: Red, yellow, etc. peppers may be substituted for the green peppers indicated. Gives color and taste variations, all delicious.

ALL-AMERICAN APPLE BUTTER

This recipe may also be made with apricots, crabapples, figs, peaches, pears or plums. Making apple butter was a very time-consuming task before this microwave method simplified the process. Makes 4 half-pint jars.

8 cups peeled, cored and chopped apples (1-inch chunks)
1 cup apple cider **or** juice
2 cups granulated sugar
1 tsp. ground cinnamon*
½ tsp. ground cloves*

Combine apples and cider in a 4-quart or larger bowl. Cover and microwave on HIGH (100%) power for 10 to 12 minutes, stirring with a wooden spoon every 3 minutes. Take cooked apples and process to a pulp consistency in a blender or food processor. Return apple pulp to mixing bowl and stir in sugar and spices. Microwave uncovered on HIGH for 15 to 20 minutes, stirring every 5 minutes. Check consistency. Butters are not as precise as jams and jellies. Give additional cooking time if necessary. Ladle hot apple butter into hot, sterile jars, leaving ¼ " headspace, seal.

• For immediate use: Let cool, refrigerate. Keeps 1 month or more.

• For longer storage: Process sealed jars conventionally in a boiling water bath for 10 minutes.

* Variation: Whole-Spice Apple Butter: If you prefer to use whole spices instead of ground, tie whole cinnamon and cloves into a muslin bag or cloth. Add at the beginning of cooking with apples and juice. Be sure to remove the bag after the first cooking step. Proceed as directed.

Tip: Spices tend to be stronger just after cooking, they will mellow after a day or two. You may adjust the recipe for your taste using less sugar or honey if you wish. This may affect cooking time.

LEMON CURD

This traditional English recipe has a sauce-like consistency. Serve this tart-sweet, creamy treat as you would any jam. It is especially good on hot scones, gingerbread or as a cake filling. Makes 1½ cups.

6 Tbsp. butter **or** margarine
¾ cup granulated sugar
2 tsp. grated lemon rind
¼ cup lemon juice
3 eggs, beaten

Place butter in a large glass measure or bowl. Microwave on HIGH (100%) power for 10 seconds or until butter is soft but not melted. Stir or whisk in sugar, lemon rind and juice. Add eggs and blend well. Cover with waxed paper and microwave on HIGH for 3 minutes, stirring every minute.

Pour mixture into a sterilized container, cover and let cool. Curd becomes thicker upon standing.

- For immediate use: Refrigerate up to 1 week.

- For longer storage: Freeze; leave 1″ headspace; use within 3 months.

Variation: LEMON CURD WITH HONEY: One-half cup of honey may be substituted for the ¾ cup sugar. Cook as directed.

Variation: LIME OR ORANGE CURD: Substitute lime or orange juice and rind for lemon. Proceed as directed.

LEMON CURD PIE OR TARTS

*This easy but superbly delicious recipe uses **Lemon Curd** as its primary ingredient. Makes one 9" pie or 6 tarts.*

One 9" baked pie shell **or** 6 tart shells*
1½ cups **Lemon Curd**, cooled
1½ cups sweetened whipped cream
thin lemon slices for garnish

In a large mixing bowl, gently fold Lemon Curd and whipped cream. Spoon into pie or tart shells. Garnish with lemon slices. Chill for one hour. Serve.

*Note: Cookie crumb, graham cracker or traditional flour crust may be used.

Variation: Sprinkle toasted coconut over whipped cream or meringue topping.

TOASTED COCONUT

Toasted coconut is easy to make in the microwave oven. Spread ½ cup flaked coconut in a pie plate or on a paper plate. Microwave on HIGH (100%) power, uncovered, for 3 to 4 minutes, stirring after 2 minutes, and every 30 seconds thereafter or until coconut turns a light golden brown.

JUICY LEMONS, LIMES OR ORANGES

To release more juice from these citrus fruits place, one at a time, in microwave oven and microwave on HIGH (100%) power for 30 seconds. Cut and squeeze fruits as usual.

APRICOT-NUT CONSERVE

This colorful and unusual conserve can be made with peaches or nectarines if you prefer. An excellent gift. Makes 6 half-pint jars.

3 cups apricots **or** peaches **or** nectarines
1 cup crushed pineapple, drained
3½ cups granulated sugar
¼ cup lemon juice **or** fruit liqueur (lemon, apricot, peach, orange)*
3 oz. liquid pectin
½ cup chopped nuts (walnuts or pecans are excellent)

Combine fruits with sugar and lemon juice, if used, in a large deep, 4 to 5 quart bowl. (If using liqueur, do not add it at this time.) Microwave on HIGH (100%) power for 15 minutes, stirring every 5 minutes. Microwave 1 to 2 minutes more to bring to a boil. Stir in liqueur. Stir in pectin and skim off any foam. Stir in nuts, ladle into hot, sterile jars, seal, and follow boiling water bath canner chart on page 44.

*Note: To make your own liqueurs, refer to **HOW TO MAKE DANISH FRUIT LIQUEURS** by Cheryl Long or **CLASSIC LIQUEURS** by Cheryl Long and Heather Kibbey.

PEELING PEACHES, NECTARINES OR APRICOTS

Bring 2 cups of water to a boil in a 4-cup glass measure on HIGH (100%) power (about 4 to 5 minutes). Spear fruit with a fork and hold it under the hot water for 30 seconds. Quickly cool fruit under cold tap water or in a bowl of ice water. Peel.

For larger quantities, increase size of container, water and microwave time. Place several whole fruits in water that has just boiled. Remove fruit after 1 minute, place in ice water, and peel. Reheat water as necessary by microwaving on HIGH until water boils.

NOTE: If fruit is under-ripe, it may need additional time in the boiling water.

Chapter Five

PICKLES, RELISHES
AND CONDIMENTS

PICKLES, RELISHES AND CONDIMENTS

Microwave preserving techniques shine in the pickle, relish and condiment chapter. Pickle brines are a cinch to make, and relishes and condiments don't require constant "pot-watching" to avoid scorching. Old-fashioned slow-cooking recipes such as **Heather's Mild Chili Sauce** and **Tomato Butter** recipes have been reduced to less than half their conventional cooking time.

When longer shelf-storage is desired, we and the U.S.D.A. Extension Service recommend a Boiling-Water Bath for pickles, relishes or condiments. Note that this process is conventional, not a microwave process.

PICKLING TIPS

Salt: When a pickle recipe calls for salt, be sure to use pure, granulated pickling salt or uniodized table salt. Pickling salt is preferred. Table salt, even uniodized, contains an anticaking ingredient that may make the brine cloudy. Iodized salt can also make pickles darken.

Vinegar: Select a high-grade vinegar from 4 to 6% acidity (40 to 60 grain). Cider vinegar is generally used for most pickles. Distilled white vinegar may be substituted for cider vinegar, especially when a lighter-colored pickled product is desired. Vinegar provides that special tangy tartness to pickles and relishes as well as acting as a preservative. **Do not dilute vinegar** — follow recipe exactly.

Sugar: Sugar balances the tartness of the vinegar. It will also give you a milder flavored pickle. If a milder pickle is desired, add sugar to the pickling solution instead of diluting the vinegar. Granulated white sugar is generally used for most pickles and is preferred for light-colored pickles. Packed brown sugar may be used for darker varieties of pickles for its special flavor.

Water: If your water is exceptionally hard, you may wish to use distilled water for better pickle making. The minerals in hard water will settle to the bottom of the jar after processing.

ENGLISH MINT SAUCE

A classic meat condiment borrowed from England. Makes about ⅔ cup.

3 Tbsp. water
2 Tbsp. sugar
⅓ cup finely chopped fresh **or** ¼ cup dried mint leaves
⅓ cup vinegar (white wine **or** champagne vinegar preferred)
green food coloring (optional)

In a 2-cup glass measure combine water and sugar. Microwave on HIGH (100%) power for 45 seconds. Stir to make sure sugar is well dissolved. Allow to cool. Add remaining ingredients. Stir well and allow to rest ½ hour before serving.

• For longer storage: Place sauce in a tightly-capped glass bottle and store at room temperature.

59

HOMESTYLE BREAD AND BUTTER PICKLES

Everyone loves these mild and fresh tasting favorites.
Makes 4 pints.

Step 1:

2½ lbs. pickling cucumbers, washed, trimmed and sliced
1 small onion, peeled and sliced into rings
ice water

Place sliced cucumbers and onion rings in a large
(4-quart or larger) bowl. Cover with ice water. Soak until
crisp, at least one hour. Microwave on HIGH (100%)
power, covered for 7 to 8 minutes or until 110° F is
reached.* Stir twice during heating time.

*Note: If you have a microwave-safe thermometer, place
in mixture and check temperature. If you have a
microwave temperature probe, place probe in center of
mixture and set temperature for 110°F. Timing is then
automatic. If you do not have either of these, check
temperature periodically with your conventional
thermometer by stopping the microwave oven and
inserting thermometer into center of mixture. Do not
leave thermometer in mixture while cooking unless it is
safe for microwave use.

Drain and pack into clean jars.

Step 2:

1½ cups cider vinegar
1½ cups water
1½ cups granulated sugar
1½ tsp. celery seed
1½ tsp. mustard seed
¾ tsp. pickling salt
¾ tsp. dill seed

Combine remaining ingredients in a large 3-quart or more mixing bowl. Microwave on HIGH for 10 minutes or until mixture comes to a full boil. Stir every 3 minutes. Pour hot mixture over cucumber and onion mixture in jars. Seal.

• For immediate use: Let age 24 to 48 hours in refrigerator before using. Keeps one month or more in refrigerator.

• For longer storage: Process pint jars conventionally in a boiling water bath for 10 minutes.

EASY CANDIED DILL PICKLES

A shortcut recipe for an old-fashioned American favorite. Makes 2 pints.

3 cups granulated sugar
⅔ cup white vinegar
2 Tbsp. mixed pickling spices
1 qt. dill pickles*

Drain dill pickles, discard liquid with spices. Cut whole pickles into strips lengthwise. Pack pickles into pint jars. Set aside until syrup is made.

Combine sugar, vinegar and spices in a large glass mixing bowl. Microwave on HIGH (100%) power for 2 minutes, stir and microwave 1 to 2 minutes more until mixture comes to a full boil. Stir. Let cool slightly.

Strain off pickling spices and pour warm syrup over pickle strips. Seal and store in refrigerator one week before using. Keeps in refrigerator.

*Note: Use regular dill, not kosher/deli dill pickles, for best results.

SWEET MIXED PICKLES

*Make classic homemade **Sweet Mixed Pickles** and keep your kitchen cool with this microwave method. Makes 3 pints.*

2 cups ½″ chunked **or** sliced pickling cucumbers
2 cups cauliflower flowerettes
1 large sweet red pepper, seeded, cut into 1″ chunks
1 cup peeled tiny onions*
¼ cup pickling salt
3 cups white **or** cider vinegar
1 cup granulated sugar
¾ cup packed light brown **or** raw sugar
¼ tsp. turmeric
1 Tbsp. mixed pickling spices
1 whole stick cinnamon, broken in half
6 whole cloves
1 tsp. mustard seed

*Note: If using frozen tiny onions, do not let stand overnight in salted water. Add as directed.

Combine vegetables and sprinkle with salt. Cover with cold water. Place lid or plastic wrap over container and refrigerate overnight.

Drain off salted water; rinse with fresh water and drain well. Combine vinegar, sugar and turmeric in a large mixing bowl. Stir to dissolve sugar. Place spices in muslin bag and add to vinegar mixture. Microwave on HIGH (100%) power for 15 to 18 minutes or until mixture comes to a boil. Stir twice during cooking time.

After mixture has reached a boil, lower power setting to MEDIUM-HIGH (70%) power and microwave for 10 minutes, stirring twice.

Add drained vegetables, (and frozen tiny onions, if used), to hot vinegar mixture. Microwave on HIGH power just until mixture comes to a boil, about 10 to 12 minutes. Remove and discard spice bag. Ladle hot pickle mixture into hot, sterile jars, leaving ½" headspace. Seal jars.

• For immediate use: Let cool and refrigerate. Keeps one month or more in refrigerator.

• For longer storage: Process sealed jars conventionally in a boiling water bath canner for 5 minutes. Check seals, cool and store.

SOFTENING BROWN SUGAR

If your box of brown sugar is hard, you can soften and freshen the brown sugar by placing the entire box in your microwave and heating it on HIGH (100%) power for about 20 seconds. (Time will vary slightly depending upon the amount of sugar in the box.)

To keep brown sugar soft, add one slice of apple peel to box or container of brown sugar. The apple peel will not spoil, but dries in the brown sugar while keeping it moist.

WATERMELON PICKLES

We developed this recipe at the request — no, insistence — of Cheryl's mother. (She loves them!) They became a new favorite with our families. (Grandmother knows best.) We hope you will like them as well as we do. Makes 3 half-pint jars.

Step 1:

5 cups peeled, cubed watermelon rind
5 cups water
¼ cup pickling salt

Remove all green or outer rind and pink inner portions from watermelon. The firm white or greenish-white layer of the watermelon is what is used. Cut into 1″ cubes. Place in a large mixing bowl and add water and salt. Stir to combine, being careful not to mash cubes. Cover; let stand overnight.

Step 2:

2 cups granulated sugar
1 cup white vinegar
Muslin spice bag containing:
      3 cinnamon sticks, broken in half
      2 tsp. whole cloves
      ½ tsp. mustard seed

Drain off salted water from cubed watermelon rind. Add warm water until watermelon rind is just covered. Microwave, covered, on HIGH (100%) power until mixture just comes to a boil (time will vary depending upon the starting temperature of the warm water). Microwave on MEDIUM-HIGH (70%) power for 2 to 3 minutes. Drain off water and set watermelon aside.

In a 2-quart mixing bowl, combine sugar and vinegar. Add spice bag and microwave on HIGH power for 4 to 5 minutes or until mixture comes to a full boil. Set aside for 15 minutes.

Add drained watermelon to liquid mixture. Microwave on HIGH power until mixture comes to a boil, about 4 to 5 minutes. Stir gently; remove and discard spice bag. Microwave on MEDIUM-HIGH power up to 5 to 6 minutes more or until fruit is clear and slightly transparent. Pack hot mixture immediately into hot sterile jars. Seal.

• For immediate use: Cool and refrigerate. Keeps several months.

• For longer storage: Process in a boiling water bath for 5 minutes.

NO-FAIL DILL PICKLES

This easy recipe hasn't failed yet! Summer-fresh dill pickles made coolly in your kitchen with a microwave assist. Makes 2 one-quart jars.

2 quarts fresh cucumbers
4 to 8 heads fresh dill, to taste
¼ cup pickling salt
3 cloves garlic, peeled and minced
1 cup vinegar
3 cups water

Wash, trim and prick cucumbers with a fork. Pack cucumbers into sterilized quart jars to within ½" of top. Sprinkle chopped dill heads and minced garlic through as you are packing jars. Set jars aside.

Combine vinegar, water and salt in a 2-quart batter bowl. Stir to combine. Microwave on HIGH (100%) power for 8 to 9 minutes or until mixture comes to a boil. Remove, stir and pour hot brine over cucumbers. Seal jars, let cool.

• For immediate use: Place cooled jars in refrigerator and let age 2 weeks before using. Store in refrigerator.

• For longer storage: Process quart jars in a boiling water bath for 15 minutes.

HELENE'S SPECIAL MUSTARD RELISH

This great relish comes from mustard expert, Helene Sawyer, author of **GOURMET MUSTARDS: HOW TO MAKE AND COOK WITH THEM.** *Perfect for hot dogs, or use in tartar sauce, etc. Chop vegetables finely so they will blend and spread easily. Fast work if you have a food processor! Makes 3 pints.*

2 cups finely chopped cabbage (about ½ small head)
2 cups finely chopped cucumbers (about 2 medium)
½ cup finely chopped onion
1 cup finely chopped sweet green pepper
1 tsp. turmeric
2 Tbsp. uniodized salt
1 qt. warm water
2 Tbsp. pickling spices
¾ cup packed brown sugar
2 cups cider vinegar
2 Tbsp. dry mustard
1½ tsp. yellow mustard seed
¼ tsp. ground ginger
½ tsp. celery seed

Combine cabbage, cucumbers, onion and pepper in a large mixing bowl; sprinkle with turmeric. Dissolve salt in warm water and pour over vegetables; let stand covered, 3 to 4 hours. Drain off salted water.

Place pickling spice in a small muslin bag. Combine bag, sugar and vinegar in a 2-quart batter or mixing bowl. Microwave on HIGH (100%) power until mixture comes to a boil; stir after 3 minutes. Add mustard, mustard seed, ginger and celery seed to vegetables; pour hot spice mixture over vegetables and stir lightly. Cover and let stand overnight in a cool place. Microwave mixture on HIGH until it comes to a boil. Remove and discard pickling spice bag. Pack hot relish into clean, hot jars, leaving ½″ headspace.

• For immediate use: Let cool and refrigerate.

• For longer storage: Process sealed jars conventionally in a boiling water bath canner for 10 minutes. Check seals, cool and store.

66

CALICO SWEET PICKLE RELISH

Traditional sweet pickle relish cooks quickly and easily in your microwave oven. Chop vegetables in the food processor to save even more time. Fresh tasting and delicious! Makes 3 pints.

3½ cups chopped pickling cucumbers (about 6 medium)
2 medium onions, peeled and chopped
1 large sweet green pepper, seeded and chopped
2 medium sweet red peppers, seeded and chopped
¼ cup pickling **or** uniodized salt
½ cup cold water
1½ cups granulated sugar
1 cup white **or** cider vinegar
1 tsp. mustard seed
1 tsp. celery seed
¼ tsp. turmeric

Combine vegetables in a large container and sprinkle with salt. Add water; stir to mix well. Place lid or plastic wrap over container and refrigerate overnight. Drain off salted water. Rinse in fresh water and drain well. In large mixing bowl, combine sugar, vinegar and spices, stirring to mix well. Microwave on HIGH (100%) power for 5 to 6 minutes or until mixture comes to a boil, stirring twice. Add the drained, chopped vegetables to the vinegar mixture, stirring well to combine. Microwave on HIGH power for 6 to 7 minutes, or until mixture comes to a boil, stirring twice. Ladle hot mixture into hot, sterile jars, leaving ½" headspace.

- For immediate use: Let cool and refrigerate.

- For longer storage: Process pint jars conventionally in a boiling water bath for 10 minutes.

ZUCCHINI RELISH

This tangy relish can be used in place of the standard pickle relish. Expect raves! Makes 4 pints.

Vegetables:

3½ to 4 cups chopped zucchini (about 3 medium, 8″ to 9″ long)
2 onions, peeled and chopped; about 2½ cups
1 green pepper, seeded, trimmed and chopped
1 red pepper, seeded, trimmed and chopped
¼ cup pickling salt
ice water

Pickling Syrup:

1½ cups granulated sugar
1¼ cups white **or** cider vinegar
⅓ cup water
1 tsp. each: celery seed and turmeric
½ tsp. mustard seed

Wash and prepare vegetables. In 6-quart or larger container, dissolve salt into enough ice water to cover vegetables. Add vegetable mixture, stir and allow to stand for 1 hour.

After standing, drain off salted water, rinse vegetables with cold water. Drain well. Set aside to complete draining as pickling syrup is prepared.

In a 4-quart or larger mixing bowl combine all ingredients for pickling syrup. Stir, then cover with plastic wrap. Microwave on HIGH power (100%) for 6 to 7 minutes, or until mixture comes to a boil. Stir, then reduce power to MEDIUM-HIGH (70%) power and microwave, uncovered, for 3 minutes.

Carefully add well-drained vegetables to pickling syrup, stirring to combine well. Microwave on HIGH for 10 minutes, or until mixture comes to a boil, stirring twice. Stir and ladle into prepared sterile jars.

• For immediate use: Cool and refrigerate jars up to 2 months.

• For longer storage: Leave ½" headspace in jars. Process sealed jars in a conventional boiling water bath for 10 minutes.

CONFETTI CORN RELISH

This delicious old-fashioned relish can be made year-round with canned corn. If using fresh or frozen corn, cook corn before preparing recipe. Good as a side dish with meat or poultry; great for picnics. Makes 3 half-pint jars.

⅓ cup granulated sugar
1 Tbsp. cornstarch
1 tsp. mustard seed
1 tsp. celery seed
¼ tsp. turmeric
½ cup chopped onion
⅓ cup chopped sweet green pepper
⅓ cup chopped sweet red pepper
2 Tbsp. corn liquid* or water
⅓ cup white **or** cider vinegar
⅓ cup pickle **or** zucchini relish
2 cups cooked corn (one 16- to 17-oz. can, drained, *reserving 2 Tbsp. liquid)

In a 2-quart glass bowl or 3-quart bowl combine all ingredients except corn, mixing well. Cover with plastic wrap and microwave on HIGH (100%) power for 3 minutes. Stir in corn. Microwave on HIGH for 4 minutes more or until mixture boils and thickens slightly. Stir and ladle into prepared sterile jars. Seal.

• For immediate use: Cool, and refrigerate up to 4 weeks.

• For longer storage: Process sealed jars in a conventional water bath canner for 15 minutes.

PICKLED VEGETABLES

Tender-crisp microwave vegetables work superbly in this dill-flavored recipe. A change of pace for the appetizer or salad buffet. Suggested vegetables: small asparagus spears, green or wax beans, baby or French carrots or cauliflower (separate into flowerettes). Makes about 2 quarts.

2 lbs. fresh vegetables, washed and trimmed

Place trimmed vegetable of choice in casserole or bowl, cover with lid or plastic wrap. Microwave on HIGH (100%) power as follows:

Asparagus: 6 to 8 minutes
spears, cut
into 2 or 3" pieces

Beans: Green and/or Wax: 10 to 12 minutes
whole or cut into
3 or 4" pieces

Carrots: French or baby: 12 to 14 minutes
whole or cut into 1"
chunks or thin sticks

Cauliflower: 7 to 9 minutes
break or cut into
flowerettes

Place cooked vegetable(s) into two 1-quart sterile jars. Set aside.

Pickling Brine:

2 cups hot water
2 cups white **or** white wine vinegar
⅔ cup granulated sugar
2 Tbsp. coarse (Kosher-style) salt
6 whole peppercorns
4 cloves fresh garlic, peeled
2 tsp. whole mustard seed
2 tsp. dill weed
¼ tsp. celery seeds

In a 2-quart batter bowl or mixing bowl combine water, vinegar, sugar and salt. Stir to combine. Microwave, covered, on HIGH (100%) power until mixture comes to a boil, about 5 to 6 minutes. Stir.

Divide spices evenly between quart jars. Pour hot vinegar mixture over vegetables. Seal and refrigerate at least 8 hours before serving. Serve chilled.

• For immediate use: Keeps in refrigerator up to 2 weeks.

• For longer storage: Process sealed jars in a conventional boiling water canner for 10 minutes. (Do not refrigerate first if processing; jars should not be cold.)

QUICK PICKLED BEETS

Spicy-sweet pickled flavor reminiscent of its Scandinavian home-style origins but updated for today's microwave cook. Makes about 1 pint.

1 (16 oz.) can sliced beets; drain and reserve liquid
⅓ cup sugar
⅓ cup vinegar
¼ tsp. salt, (optional)
4 whole cloves
4 whole allspice
½″ stick cinnamon
½ tsp. dried minced onion

In a 2-quart glass batter bowl or mixing bowl, combine all ingredients including reserved beet liquid, except sliced beets. Microwave on HIGH (100%) power for 4 to 5 minutes or until mixture comes to a full boil, stirring once halfway through cooking time. Remove from microwave and add drained sliced beets to liquid mixture, stir gently. Refrigerate in a covered container 12 to 24 hours before removing whole spices and serving. Serve chilled. Keeps 3 to 4 weeks in the refrigerator.

HEATHER'S MILD CHILI SAUCE

Heather Kibbey, editor of Oregon Restaurateur magazine, shared this great family recipe. The chunky, but juicy, chili sauce is mild, in the English tradition. Thanks to microwave techniques, this recipe produces an even fresher taste than the original. Makes 4 pints.

4 lbs. ripe tomatoes, peeled and coarsely chopped
1 large onion, finely chopped into ¼" pieces
1 cup finely chopped celery
½ sweet green pepper, chopped
½ sweet red pepper, chopped
1 medium, firm apple, peeled, seeded and chopped
2 tsp. pickling salt **or** uniodized salt
1 rounded Tbsp. pickling spices, tied in a muslin bag
⅔ cup granulated sugar
⅔ cup white vinegar

In a large (4-quart or larger) mixing bowl, combine all ingredients. Microwave on HIGH power for 35 minutes, stirring every 5 to 10 minutes. Remove and discord spice bag. Ladle hot mixture into hot, sterile jars and seal.

• For immediate use: Let cool and refrigerate. Best after 24 hours.

• For longer storage: Process sealed jars in a conventional water bath canner for 15 minutes.

PEELING TOMATOES

Bring 2 cups of water to a boil in a 4-cup glass measure on HIGH (100%) power (about 4 to 5 minutes). Spear tomato with a fork and hold it under the hot water for 12 to 15 seconds. Quickly cool tomato under cold tap water or in a bowl of ice water. Peel.

For larger quantities, increase size of container, water and microwave time. Place several whole tomatoes in water that has just boiled. Remove tomatoes after 20 to 25 seconds, place in ice water, and peel. Reheat water as necessary by microwaving on HIGH until water boils.

SPICY AMERICAN BARBECUE SAUCE

A versatile barbecue sauce that's a perfect complement for meats and poultry. Quick, easy-to-make and economical too! Makes 1 pint.

½ cup chopped onion
1 clove peeled, minced garlic, optional
1 (8-oz.) can tomato sauce
½ cup chili sauce
½ tsp. dry mustard
1 Tbsp. molasses
2 Tbsp. brown sugar
¼ tsp. paprika
¼ tsp. salt
⅛ tsp. pepper
dash Tabasco sauce
2 tsp. Worcestershire sauce
2 Tbsp. lemon juice **or** vinegar

Place onions and garlic in a 4-cup glass measure. cover with plastic wrap. Microwave on HIGH (100%) power for 3 minutes. Stir in all remaining ingredients and microwave, uncovered, on HIGH for 5 minutes, stirring twice.

• For immediate use: Ladle into desired jar or container. Seal or cover, and refrigerate.

• For longer storage: Pack into freezer containers, leaving 1″ headspace; freeze.

• To can: Pack into hot, sterile jars while sauce is hot. Process sealed jars conventionally in a boiling water bath for 15 minutes.

TOMATO BUTTER

A wonderful family heirloom family recipe from our food-wise friend, Heather Kibbey. We've updated the recipe for microwave cooking. Do try this as a meat condiment or use as you would catsup or chili sauce. Definitely gourmet, definitely superb! Makes 4 pints.

5 lbs. ripe tomatoes, peeled and sliced
2 cups cider vinegar
1½ tsp. salt
2¾ cups packed light brown sugar
¼ cup plus 1 Tbsp. pickling spices
3 Tbsp. cornstarch
3 Tbsp. water

In a 4-quart or larger mixing bowl place peeled, sliced tomatoes and vinegar; stir and cover. Let stand overnight.

Process tomato mixture in a blender or food processor to purée. (You may need to do this in small batches.) Return puréed mixture to mixing bowl and add salt, stirring well. Microwave on HIGH (100%) power for 40 minutes, stirring every 10 minutes.

Place spice in muslin bag. Add brown sugar to puréed mixture, stirring well. Add spice bag to mixture. Microwave on HIGH for 40 minutes, stirring every 5 to 10 minutes.

Remove and discard spice bag. Combine cornstarch and water in a measuring cup, stirring until smooth. Add a small amuount of the hot tomato mixture, one spoonful at a time, to the cornstarch mixture; stirring well. Add cornstarch mixture to larger hot mixture; stirring well. Microwave on HIGH for 5 minutes, stir well. Ladle into sterile, hot containers, leaving ½" headspace; seal.

• For immediate use: Let cool and refrigerate. Keeps a month or more.

• For longer storage: Process sealed pints conventionally in a boiling water bath for 15 minutes. Check seals, cool and store.

OREGON CRANBERRY CHUTNEY

Marsha Peters Johnson, author of HOW TO MAKE AND COOK WITH GOURMET VINEGARS, shares this exquisite recipe which we adapted for microwave convenience. This beautiful, spicy, garnet-colored chutney is perfect with roasted meats, poultry, cream cheese or crackers. A quick gourmet gift. Makes 5-6 half-pints.

2 cups whole cranberries, ground in blender **or** food processor
1 cup white, apple cider, white wine **or** cranberry vinegar*
2 cups granulated sugar
2 tsp. ground ginger
1 tsp. ground cloves
¼ tsp. chili powder
5 to 6 drops hot pepper sauce
1 tsp. salt
2 garlic cloves, minced
3 to 4 medium tart apples; peeled, cored and diced (about 4 to 5 cups)
1 cup chopped nuts (almonds, pecans **or** walnuts)

Finely chop cranberries in blender or food processor, adding ¼ cup of the vinegar. Combine first nine ingredients in a 2-quart glass batter bowl or 3-quart deep bowl. Microwave on HIGH (100%) power for 3 minutes. Stir; continue to microwave on HIGH until mixture comes to a boil (about 4 to 6 minutes). Stir in diced apples. Microwave on MEDIUM-HIGH (70%) power for 13 minutes, stirring twice to cook fruit evenly. Check consistency, mixture should be thick and evenly cooked. Add nuts, stir to mix well. Ladle into sterile containers.

• For immediate use: Refrigerate up to 4 weeks.

• For longer storage: Freeze; leave 1″ headspace, up to 6 months.

• To can: Pack into hot, sterile jars. Leave ½″ headspace. Process half-pint jars conventionally in a boiling water bath for 10 minutes.

*Note: To make Cranberry Vinegar, and other gourmet vinegars, refer to **HOW TO MAKE AND COOK WITH GOURMET VINEGARS** by Marsha Peters Johnson.

EASY SALSA

This medium-hot salsa recipe can be made at any time of the year. If you prefer it milder or hotter, just vary the amount of jalapeño chilis accordingly. Makes about 3 pints.

1 large can (28 oz.) whole pack tomatoes
2 medium onions, peeled and chopped
1 tsp. garlic powder
3 Tbsp. vegetable oil
2 Tbsp. white **or** white wine vinegar
1 tsp. ground cumin
dash salt and pepper
2 (4 oz.) cans chopped green chilis
1 (4 oz.) can chopped jalapeño chilis

Coarsely chop tomatoes. In large mixing bowl combine onions and vegetable oil. Sauté on HIGH (100%) power for 4 minutes, stirring several times. Add all remaining ingredients to sautéed onions, stirring to combine well. Microwave on HIGH for 3 minutes, then reduce power to MEDIUM (50%) power and simmer for 20 minutes, stirring occasionally.

• For immediate use: Cool to room temperature and serve or refrigerate up to 2 weeks.

• For longer storage: Let cool and pack into freezer containers, leaving ½" headspace; freeze up to 6 months.

FRESH SALSA VERDE

Salsa Verde is the Spanish name for "green sauce". So good on chicken or crab enchiladas as well as other Mexican dishes. Makes 1 pint.

1 lb. fresh tomatillos
¾ cup chopped onion
1 sweet green pepper
1 **or** 2 fresh jalapeño chilies*
2 Tbsp. fresh cilantro leaves
2 cloves garlic, peeled
½ tsp. granulated sugar

Peel tomatillos. Place tomatillos in a 3-quart or larger mixing bowl and cover with warm water. Microwave on HIGH (100%) power until mixture comes up to a boil. (Time will vary depending upon the starting temperature of the water.) Reduce power to MEDIUM-HIGH (70%) and microwave for 3 minutes. Drain off water.

Wash, trim and seed pepper and chilies. Coarsely chop tomatillos, pepper, chilies and garlic. Combine all ingredients in a food processor or blender. If too thick add water one teaspoon at a time. Chop finely to sauce consistency. Pour into covered container. Refrigerate at least 1 hour for flavors to blend. Refrigerate sauce. Keeps up to 1 week.

*Note: Vary the number of jalapeño chilies depending upon the hotness desired: use one chili for medium, two for hot. If you like a very mild salsa, substitute 1 large fresh or 2 canned green chilies.

EGGPLANT CAPONATA

Caponata is an Italian eggplant appetizer that is also an excellent meat accompaniment. Serve chilled or at room temperature with crackers or French or Italian bread. Makes about 4 pints.

Step 1:
3 large onions, coarsely chopped
2 large green bell peppers, seeded and coarsely chopped
1½ cups chopped celery
½ cup olive oil

Combine vegetables and olive oil in a 4-quart or larger bowl. Cover with plastic wrap. Microwave on HIGH (100%) power for 10 minutes, stirring halfway through. Reduce power to MEDIUM (50%) power and cook for 10 more minutes, stirring occasionally.

Step 2:
2 large eggplants, cut into ½" cubes
1 (8 oz.) can tomato sauce
1 (6 oz.) can tomato paste

If preferred, soak eggplant cubes in lightly salted water, drain. Add eggplant to sautéed onion mixture: stir. Microwave on HIGH for 30 minutes, stirring every 10 minutes. Add tomato sauce and paste, stirring to combine well. Microwave 10 minutes on HIGH.

Step 3:
4 cloves garlic peeled and minced
½ cup pitted black olives
½ cup pitted green olives, (regular **or** stuffed)
½ cup red wine vinegar
3 Tbsp. granulated sugar
1 (3 oz.) jar capers
1½ tsp. dried oregano
1 tsp. salt, optional
1 tsp. pepper
1 tsp. dried basil

Stir in all remaining ingredients. Microwave on HIGH power for 5 minutes.

• For immediate use: Cool to room temperature and serve or refrigerate up to 1 week.

• For longer storage: Let cool and pack in freezer containers, leaving ½" headspace, freeze up to 6 months.

ROASTED PUMPKIN SEEDS

Here's a lively condiment for salads, vegetables and casseroles. Try this recipe also with Danish or butternut squash seeds — crunchy and delicious! Makes about 1 cup.

1 cup raw pumpkin seeds
salt
½ tsp. oil (optional)

Rinse fibers from pumpkin seeds; drain. Sprinkle a light coating of salt on a microwave baking tray or shallow dish. Place damp seeds in a single layer on the salt. Drizzle ½ teaspoon oil over seeds, if desired. Microwave uncovered on HIGH (100%) power for 6 to 7 minutes, stirring once halfway through cooking time. Taste test seeds for crispness. Add 1 to 2 minutes more if needed. Store in a sealed container.

MARINATED MUSHROOMS

An extremely popular appetizer or salad accompaniment that is a weight-watchers delight! Makes 1 quart.

1 lb. fresh whole small mushrooms
1 small onion, peeled and sliced
1 Tbsp. olive oil

Pickling brine:
⅔ cup white wine **or** white **or** cider vinegar
⅓ cup water
1½ tsp. pickling **or** uniodized salt
1 tsp. fresh **or** ½ tsp. dried chervil **or** parsley flakes
1 bay leaf
8 peppercorns

Clean mushrooms and trim stem ends. Place mushrooms and sliced onions in a large mixing bowl. Cover with plastic wrap. Microwave on HIGH (100%) power for 2 minutes, stir and recover. Microwave on HIGH for 2 minutes more. Drizzle olive oil over mushrooms; stir gently to coat mushrooms. Place in clean quart jar.

Combine all pickling brine ingredients in a 4-cup glass measure. Microwave on HIGH, 4 minutes or until mixture comes to a boil. Pour hot mixture over mushrooms. Seal jar and let cool before refrigerating. Let marinate in refrigerator for 24 hours before serving. Serve drained with bay leaf and peppercorns removed. Keeps 1 week in refrigerator.

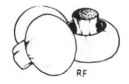

RF

Chapter Six

BEVERAGES AND
SPECIAL EXTRAS

BEVERAGES AND SPECIAL EXTRAS

This is perhaps our most creative and unique chapter. Here you'll find such special delights as: **White Chocolate-Hazelnut Heaven** and **Creamy Russian Tea Base**, to name just a few. Keep these in your freezer, ready for company or special moments as fast as your microwave can heat them.

The microwave oven is a moist-cooking appliance and therefore does not dry foods well. This, of course, is an advantage in everyday cooking. There are, however, a few exceptions, where the microwave "dries" very well. This is in drying small foods such as herbs, peels and croutons. Enjoy making your own **Bouquet Garni** and **Fines Herbes** from microwave dried herbs.

DRYING HERBS

A number of herbs such as basil, celery leaves, chervil, chives, dill, mint, oregano, parsley, sage, tarragon or thyme, may be quickly dried in your microwave oven.

1 small bunch fresh herbs (about 4 to 5 stalks)

Discard any discolored or decayed leaves. Rinse herbs in cold water; shake off excess. Pat completely dry.

Place a double layer of paper towels* in microwave. Spread herbs on paper towels. Place another paper towel over herbs. Microwave on HIGH (100%) power for 2 to 3 minutes. Check leaves for dryness by rubbing between paper towels to crumble. If leaves are not dry, microwave an additional 30 seconds at a time until dry. Remove from microwave and allow to cool. Crumble herbs, discard any tough stems, and store in an air-tight container.

*Note: Do not use recycled paper towels.

FINES HERBES

A delicate blend of herbs suitable for sauces, cream soups, stocks, chicken, fish chowders and cheese and egg dishes. A gourmet giftable!

Blend equal amounts of dried chervil, chives, parsley, and tarragon. Place 1 or 2 teaspoons of mixture in a small muslin bag or a square of cheesecloth tied with kitchen string. Loop string for easy removal after cooking. Place bags in a dry air-tight jar and store until needed.

BOUQUET GARNI

These flavorful herb packets are treasures in your soups or stews. A great gourmet gift! Makes 4 bags.

Mix together:
2 Tbsp. each dried basil, marjoram, parsley, thyme
1 Tbsp. coarsely crushed bay leaves
8 cracked black peppercorns

Place about 2 teaspoons of mixture in a small muslin bag or a square of cheesecloth tied with kitchen string. Loop string for easy removal after cooking. Place bags in a dry air-tight jar and store until needed.

BASIC CROUTONS

Vary the taste of your croutons by using different types of bread such as French, sourdough, whole wheat, rye, etc. Makes 3 cups.

3 cups fresh ½-inch bread cubes, trimmed
2 to 3 Tbsp. oil **or** melted butter or margarine

Line a 2- to 3-quart glass baking dish with paper towels. Spread bread cubes over paper towels evenly in a single layer. Microwave on HIGH (100%) power for 2 minutes. Stir to rearrange bread cubes and continue to cook for 1 to 2 minutes more, checking and stirrinhg every 30 seconds. Remove from microwave and let stand, uncovered, until cool. Check croutons for crispness. If necessary, cook in additional 30-second increments until crisp.

Remove paper towels and drizzle oil or melted butter over croutons. Stir to coat evenly. Serve or store in an air-tight container.

Variations:
Low-Sodium, Low-Fat Croutons: Substitute low-sodium bread and omit oil, butter or margarine. Follow **BASIC CROUTON** directions.

Cheese-Garlic Croutons: Combine 3 Tbsp. Parmesan cheese with ¼ to ½ tsp. garlic powder, set aside. Follow **BASIC CROUTON** directions. Then sprinkle cheese-garlic mixture over croutons and stir well to coat evenly.

Herbed Croutons: A wide variety of dried herb mixtures can be used for this variation. Some herbs that work well are: basil, chervil, chives, marjoram, oregano, parsley, tarragon or thyme. You may wish to add garlic or onion powder to your herb mixture. Use 1 teaspoon herbs per cup of bread cubes. Follow **BASIC CROUTON** directions. Add oil as directed, then immediately add herbs and stir to coat evenly.

FESTIVE CHEESE CROCK

An easy make-ahead appetizer for entertaining. Use fresh or microwave dried herbs in the herb variation. The flavor improves with aging, but it may be used immediately. Serve with fresh round vegetable slices or crackers. Makes about 1 pint.

4 cups (1 lb.) grated medium **or** sharp cheese
6 oz. cream cheese
2 Tbsp. brandy **or** port wine
2 Tbsp. olive oil
½ tsp. garlic powder
1 tsp. dry mustard
½ to 1 tsp. olive oil

Place cheese in a large glass bowl. Microwave 4 to 6 minutes on MEDIUM (50%) power or until soft, stirring after 2 minutes. Stir in the remaining ingredients, except the ½ to 1 teaspoon olive oil. Beat with a mixer until thoroughly blended. Pour reserved olive oil into crock. Spread evenly over crock interior. Pack cheese mixture into crock and cover with a tight-fitting lid. Refrigerate one week to age before serving. Serve at room temperature. Store in refrigerator.

Variation: HERBED FESTIVE CHEESE CROCK

Suggested herbs: Basil, Chervil, Chives, Cilantro, Fines Herbes or Parsley.

Layer fresh or dried herbs onto cheese mixture when packing into crock. Divide cheese mixture into three equal amounts. Place first layer into crock, pat down evenly. Place 1 teaspoon dried herbs or about that amount of fresh herbs, leaves or sprigs over top of cheese. Repeat ending with herbs on top. Place ½ teaspoon olive oil over top of herbs. Cover and refrigerate as directed.

CRANBERRY TEA

This colorful, caffeine-free "tea" is a year-round favorite whether served in a hot, steaming mug or in a tall iced glass. Makes 4 to 8 servings.

1 (12-oz.) bag fresh **or** frozen* cranberries
½ fresh orange, cut into chunks (optional)
3 cinnamon sticks
8 whole cloves
3 whole allspice

Place cranberries and orange chunks in a large casserole or bowl. Cover with hot tap water. Add spices and cover with lid or plastic wrap. Microwave on HIGH (100%) power for 5 minutes or until water comes to a boil. Stir, recover, and microwave on MEDIUM-HIGH (70%) power for 10 minutes. Pour cranberry mixture through a fine strainer into a large pitcher. Discard fruit and spices.

Add to cranberry concentrate:
1 small (6-oz.) can frozen orange juice concentrate
1 small (6-oz.) can frozen lemonade concentrate
½ cup granulated sugar

Stir to combine. Refrigerate for 24 hours before serving. Can be frozen for longer storage.

• To serve hot: Fill cup or mug with equal parts HOT water and **CRANBERRY TEA** concentrate.

•To serve cold: Fill tall 8- to 10-ounce glass with ice cubes. Pour chilled **CRANBERRY TEA** concentrate over cubes and serve. Cranberry tea concentrate may be further diluted with cold water if fewer ice cubes are preferred.

*Note: Frozen cranberries will take longer to come to a boil.

CREAMY RUSSIAN TEA BASE

A tangy, creamy, and not-so-sweet variation of the classic Russian Tea. Keep this recipe in your freezer. Makes 12 to 14 servings.

1 pint (2 cups) vanilla ice cream **or** ice milk
1 small (6-oz.) can frozen orange juice concentrate
½ cup instant tea
½ cup granulated sugar
1 tsp. ground cinnamon
½ tsp. ground cloves

Soften hard frozen ice cream, in paper carton or large bowl on WARM (10%) power for 2 to 2½ minutes. In a large mixing bowl place orange juice concentrate, tea, sugar and spices. Beat with electric mixer until well combined. Quickly beat softened ice cream into orange juice mixture until well blended. Spoon into freezer container, seal tightly, date and label. Hold in freezer until needed.
• To serve: Spoon ¼ cup Creamy Russian Tea Mix into 6- to 8-ounce mug or cup. Fill with boiling water. Stir and serve.

SWEETENED CONDENSED MILK

Make your own for a fraction of the cost! Makes 1¾ cups.

1½ cups granulated sugar
½ cup water
½ cup (1 stick) butter **or** margarine
¼ tsp. vanilla extract
2 cups instant dry milk

In a 1-quart glass measure or bowl, combine sugar, water and butter. Microwave on HIGH for 3½ to 4 minutes or until mixture comes to a boil. Stir every minute. Blend in vanilla and dry milk. Beat well until smooth in a blender, food processor or using a mixer. Let cool. Store covered in refrigerator.

HOT BUTTERED RUM BASE

A classic hot drink with a creamy twist. Makes about 20 to 25 servings.

1 pint (2 cups) vanilla ice cream **or** ice milk
1 cup butter **or** margarine
1 cup brown sugar
2 tsp. ground cinnamon
½ tsp. ground nutmeg

Soften hard frozen ice cream in paper carton or large bowl on WARM (10%) power for 2 to 2½ minutes. Set aside.

In large mixing bowl soften butter on WARM (10%) power for 3 to 4 minutes. Add brown sugar, cinnamon, and nutmeg to softened butter. Beat mixture with electric mixer until well combined and fluffy. Quickly add softened ice cream and continue to beat until well mixed. Spoon into freezer container, seal tightly, date and label. Hold in freezer until needed. This mixture wil not freeze solid.

• To serve: Place 2 to 3 rounded tablespoons **HOT BUTTERED RUM BASE** in cup or mug. Add 2 to 3 tablespoons rum or ¼ teaspoon rum extract, if desired. Pour boiling water over all, stirring well to combine. Serve immediately.

RICH HOT CHOCOLATE BASE

This quick and easy basic hot chocolate recipe is a versatile performer. From your freezer base it can be transformed into five different and delicious hot beverages. Makes about 18 servings.

1 pint (2 cups) vanilla ice cream **or** ice milk
½ cup unsweetened powdered cocoa
2½ cups powdered sugar
½ cup powdered non-dairy creamer

Soften hard frozen ice cream in paper carton or large bowl on WARM (10%) power for 2 to 2½ minutes. Add remaining ingredients to softened ice cream and beat well with electric mixer. Transfer to freezer container. Freeze until ready to serve.

• To serve: Place 2 to 3 tablespoons **RICH HOT CHOCOLATE BASE** in a 6- to 8-ounce cup or mug. Fill with boiling water and stir. Top with marshmallow or whipped cream if desired.

Base Variations:

CINNAMON HOT CHOCOLATE: To RICH HOT CHOCOLATE BASE recipe add 2 teaspoons ground cinnamon and proceed as directed.

MINT HOT CHOCOLATE: To RICH HOT CHOCOLATE BASE recipe add 2 teaspoons mint extract and proceed as directed.

Serving Variations:

CHOCOLATE-MINT DESSERT COFFEE: Use **CINNAMON HOT CHOCOLATE BASE** recipe, substituting hot coffee for boiling water when preparing individual servings. Elegant when topped with sweetened whipped cream.

MOCHA DESSERT COFFEE: Use **CINNAMON HOT CHOCOLATE BASE** recipe, substituting hot coffee for boiling water when preparing individual servings. Garnish with sweetened whipped cream lightly dusted with ground cinnamon.

WHITE CHOCOLATE-HAZELNUT HEAVEN

A stunning and versatile recipe, which can be used as a fondue, drizzle topping, paté or, if allowed to harden, a confection. For a heavenly fondue, serve fresh fruits for dipping (especially good with fresh berries). Design a fruit plate and drizzle over for a spectacular dessert. To serve as a paté, let cool to firm and spread onto firm fruits, fruit slices, or specialty breads. To make an elegant confection, dip whole small fruits such as strawberries or cherries with stems attached, into hot fondue. Place on plate and chill until firm. Serve chilled. Easy to make and ready at a moment's notice from your freezer. Hazelnuts are also known as filberts. Makes about 4 cups.

3 cups (14 oz.) white chocolate chips **or** finely chopped
    white chocolate
¾ cup whipping cream **or** half and half
½ cup finely chopped toasted hazelnuts
1 Tbsp. hazelnut liqueur **or** 1½ tsp. almond **or** black
    walnut extract
½ tsp. vanilla extract

Place cream into a one-cup glass measure, set aside. Put white chocolate into a 2-quart glass batter or mixing bowl and microwave for 1 minute on HIGH (100%) power. Set aside.

Microwave cream on HIGH for 1 to 1 1/2 minutes or just until cream reaches a boil. While cream is being micro-waved, stir white chocolate to blend. Pour hot cream over melted chocolate. Stir in hazelnuts, liqueur or extract and vanilla. Stir to mix well.

• For immediate use: Pour into container(s) and refrigerate up to 4 weeks.

• For longer storage: Freeze, leaving ½" headspace.

INDEX

Jams and Jellies

Pickles, Relishes And Condiments

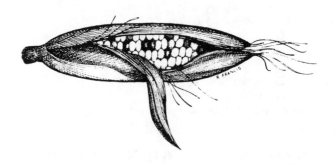

ORDER FORM

CULINARY ARTS LTD.
Publishers of Fine Specialty Cookbooks
P.O. Box 2157, Lake Oswego, Oregon 97035   (503) 639-4549

Introducing our unique and exciting
line of cookbooks and labels.

Cookbooks:

☐ **Easy Microwave Preserving**
By Cynthia Fischborn and Cheryl Long
This 96-page softcover cookbook is indexed.
ISBN# 0–914667–08–4   (paperbound) $7.95

☐ **Gourmet Mustards: How To Make And Cook With Them**
By Helene Sawyer
This 64–page softcover cookbook is indexed.
ISBN# 0–914667–07–6   (paperbound) $4.95

☐ **Gourmet Vinegars: How To Make And Cook With Them**
By Marsha Peters Johnson
This 64–page softcover cookbook is indexed.
ISBN# 0–914667–05–X   (paperbound) $4.95

☐ **How To Make Danish Fruit Liqueurs**
By Cheryl Long
This 80–page softcover cookbook is indexed.
ISBN# 0–914667–03–3   (paperbound) $5.95

☐ **Classic Liqueurs: The Art Of Making And Cooking**
With Liqueurs By Cheryl Long and Heather Kibbey'
This 112-page cookbook is indexed.
ISBN# 0–914667–11-4   (paperbound) $8.95

Labels:

12 colorful peel-and-stick labels: $1.95

☐ **Microwave Preserving,** red on white, all-purpose
☐ **Microwave Preserving, Gift,** red on white, for gifts
☐ **Gourmet Mustard,** yellow with black, all-purpose
☐ **A Gourmet Vinegar,** red on white, all-purpose
☐ **A Gift of Gourmet Vinegar,** green on white, for gifts
☐ **Liqueur Log,** blue on white, for liqueur-making
☐ **A Classic Liqueur,** green on white, all-purpose
☐ **A Gift of Liqueur,** red on white, for gifts

Please send the following quantities:

Cookbooks:

Easy Microwave Preserving _____

Gourmet Mustards _____

Gourmet Vinegars _____

Classic Liqueurs_____

Danish Fruit Liqueurs _____

Labels:

Microwave Preserving _____

Microwave Preserving Gift _____

Gourmet Mustard _____

A Gourmet Vinegar _____

A Gift of Gourmet Vinegar _____

Liqueur Log _____

A Classic Liqueur _____

A Gift of Liqueur _____

Check/money order $_____

[MasterCard] #_____   Exp. date _____

[VISA] #_____

Signature _____

Name_____

Address_____

City_____State_____Zip Code_____

Shipping: Add $1.00 for postage and handling.

CULINARY ARTS LTD.
P.O. Box 2157, Lake Oswego, Oregon 97035